Branching Out

Replicating High-Performance Field Operations

by

Frank Troppe
Chief Branchologist, 3PR Corporation
Founder, Branch Productivity Institute

*Dan —
Congrats on your continued
success!*
Frank J. Troppe

I

A SuccessDNA Nonfiction Book

Page design by Kevin Stock, KLS Image Support
Cover design by Milan Sperka and Tammy Ackerman, Mesh Creative, Inc.

SuccessDNA, Inc.
COPYRIGHT © 2004, Frank Troppe
All rights reserved
Printed in the United States of America
10 9 8 7 6 5 4 3 2 1

Library of Congress Catalog Card Number: in progress
ISBN# 0-9746844-3-0

 SUCCESS **DNA** is a trademark of SuccessDNA, Inc.

What You Will Learn in <u>Branching Out</u>...

- Where and how to find the right balance between brand compliance and local-decision making.

- The exponential value of repeating core, high-value activities in different places at the same time.

- How to use common goals to get beyond the local complaint that, "We're different." What reasons do we all share for being here?

- The common obstacles (Vices!) preventing field organizations from achieving their common goals.

- The 6 Virtues of high-performance in the field: measurable differences that distinguish high-performing field locations from their brethren stuck "in the middle" or below.

- The Cause & Effect relationship between Projective & Reflective Virtues.

- How to create a culture of meaningful learning through Your Branch University.

- How to <u>Branch Out</u> with confidence...and a plan.

The field operation is closer to its customers than the remote corporate location supporting it.

Acknowledgments

In addition to the chapter contributors named within the book, I would like to thank the following individuals for sharing their field experiences:

Steve Bilt, CEO, Bright Now! Dental
Tina Brock McCoy, Branch Manager, Venturi Partners
Charles Butler, Founder, Brookhaven, LLC
Bill Cahalan, President (Northeast), Venturi Partners
Steve Chaloupka, President SFC Business Services (formerly with Fluor Corp & Inchcape Environmental Labs)
Skip Daynes, President, Daynes Music
Nora Dool
Mark Elston, Senior Managing Director, Wachovia Securities
Mark Galloway, President, Wire the Market, Inc.
Judy Gambino, Safety Engineering Consultant, Travelers
Fred Herbert, President, RemX Financial Staffing
Erin Holley
Rick Huttner, Principal, Huttner & Associates
Kathryn Hynes
Jeff Jackovich, President, Accounting Principals
Robin Johnson, Regional Director, Technisource Inc.
Jerry Hoium, VP and Branch Manager, Modis
Chris Kilpatrick, VP, CDI Corporation
Ron Malone, President of Gentiva Health
Ray Marcy, former President of Spherion
Mark McCormick, Territory Manager – Middle Market, IBM
Maddy McPherson, District Manager, Roth Staffing
Gail Painter, Customer Service Consultant
Greg Palmer, CEO, Remedy Temp
David Pearson, VP of Channel Sales, Miller Heiman
Janice Pereira, former Managing Director, Lee Hecht Harrison
Ben Roth, CEO, Roth Staffing
Leslie Smyth, Director of Marketing & Sales, MD Hydraulics, Inc.
Garrett Sutton, President, SuccessDNA, Inc.
Joe Thiel, Managing Director – Financial Services, TEK Systems
Tom Traficanti, SVP, Heritage Bank of Nevada
Pat Troppe, Product Manager, Costar
Joseph A. Turano, III, CEO, Providus, Inc.
Jeffrey Weinstock, Managing Director, Kelly Law Registry
Ursula Williams, VP Marketing Operations Training, Accountants Inc. & ACSYS Inc.

Table of Contents

Introduction

Section I – Rethinking Branch Strategy

Section II – Achieving the Projective Virtues

Discipline

Environment

Innovation

Section III – The Next Generation

Introduction

I can't remember the last time I bought a product directly from the manufacturer's headquarters. Can you?

And how often do we receive a service directly from the "home office" of the service provider upon which they are relying?

It happens occasionally. But the vast majority of our experience as consumers, both personal and commercial, occurs via "field locations" of the manufacturer or service provider. These field locations are the channels by which most companies go to market.

Likewise, unless we are employed by a very small company, the odds are good that we work in the field, as opposed to being at "headquarters."

Stores, branches, and other types of footprint, are generally referred to as field operations. This type of infrastructure is chosen when companies want to put inventory, sales activity, service resources and/or decision-making closer to their customers. The challenge in doing that...for every mile you move closer to a customer, you put a mile between your own people.

Interviews with field employees show that the distance from home office is often perceived as an advantage. And customers certainly prefer (or insist on) local contacts. But as anyone who has worked in a geographically distributed infrastructure can attest, there are challenges in this operating model as well...

- **How do you build a healthy, vigorous culture when your people are geographically dispersed?**

- **How do you balance compliance with creativity over multiple locations?**

- **How much of your message survives the journey to each of your field operations...and how many of their messages make it back intact to corporate?**

- **What is it about the branch[1] model that, despite its cost, makes it the preferred method of going to market for so many companies?**

Background

When I was a young salesman in Chicago, I received my first assignment as a Branch Manager. I opened a local office for a global service company – and was one of literally hundreds to hold that position. About two years later, our brand new office was named the "Model Office – U.S. Operations" for that same company. How did that office grow from zero revenue into one of the top-producing locations in the service network? What does that top office have in common with other high-performance branches and stores? How do high-performing branch locations differ from their peers?

These questions are answered in Branching Out, which seeks to outline the key differences within branch office peer groups. If a vertical market is defined by industry or sector, and a horizontal market by local geography, what about the business of running branch operations? We call the 3+ million "remote site locations" operated in the U.S. a Diagonal Market. To optimize branch performance, and organizational performance, we need to revolutionize the way companies look at branch and store operations. The company I founded, 3PR Corporation, is the world's first company to focus exclusively on the needs of branch-based businesses – that's all we do.

Today, when Company X seeks to hire or promote a branch manager, Company X may closely examine the applicant's level of (a) industry experience, (b) functional experience (how good they are at "sales" or "customer service"), and/or (c) geographic experience (how well they "know this market"). Noticeably absent is a standardized inquiry into each applicant's "branch history," that is, the applicant's specific experience related to Discipline, Environment and Innovation within other branch operating structures.

Sadly, that is why many branch professionals get trapped in underperforming operations – they not only lack the access to best practices within their own company (their words, not ours!), but more importantly, from within other branch environments. It's like asking a local doctor to limit his or her professional development to the methods "that we use here at the Jones Practice." This is a problem of tribalism – and branch personnel want to see it fixed.

Our research began addressing that problem by conducting a series of personal interviews with branch managers, salespeople, service teams, and branch business executives – some had responsibility for one branch, some had responsibility for thousands. The goal of the inquiry was to establish whether best branch practices were limited by company or industry. Or whether the model a company used for its branch and store operations could also be a source of best practices so sound that they applied universally, even outside of one's own industry.

The first question: "What is a branch?" ___A branch is the local reflection of a brand's Discipline, Environment and Innovation. As an operating unit, it is always closer to the customers than the remote corporate location supporting it.___ So an American company's call-center located in India is not a branch! That call center is an example of resources being placed further from the customer solely to gain cost efficiencies. For purposes of this research, a branch is any operating unit, whether franchised or company-owned, whether retail store or B2B that is placed closer to customers than the corporate office.

A series of subsequent questions explored the following territory:

• Why does your company operate via field locations?
• Are there any goals for your company's branches that you think would be shared by other companies, even those outside your industry?
• What obstacles prevent your branches from achieving their goals?
• Describe the top-performing location in your company's network of operations.
• How does that top-performing location differ from the offices in the middle-of-the-pack?
• Have you succeeded at putting resources and decision-making closer to the customer through your field operations?

The people working in branch offices, whose careers and lifestyles depended on their performance in the branch setting, were candid and articulate with their responses. Once they answered these questions, we analyzed the answers and looked for common ground among the branches, regardless of industry or location. This book provides an inside look at those branch operations.

Let's start by considering a timeless story about a good branch gone bad...

Section I:
Rethinking Branch Strategy

Chapter One:
Requiem from the Branch Graveyard

Two thousand years ago, a young girl named Lele walked from her village into the desert…it was the first time she had entered into the world. Everything she knew about the world, she had learned in her home village.

Lele embarked on this journey with her father, who was a wise and moderately successful trader. With each and every step in the sand, Lele's senses gave up a small part of her home base. First she could no longer touch her village, and then she could no longer smell it. The shouts of well-wishers died away and she could no longer hear it. Cresting dunes soon blocked the sight of the homes, and as lunch was finished – just four hours into the journey, she could no longer taste her home. The bread she unwrapped and chewed was gritty – it already seemed more a part of this sandy wasteland than a part of her home.

Many hours later and miles away from her friends, the earth grew still. It was at this time that she stopped thinking about home and started looking around her current surroundings. In the distance, a mild wind blew sand swirls around the remains of a primitive, mysterious structure.

As they approached these remains, Lele asked, "What was this place, father?"

He replied, "This was one of seven sites where an ancient kingdom gathered. They once controlled this entire land."

As the father and daughter removed their packs and crouched to examine a pottery shard, the ghostly remains of the kingdom tried to speak to them through it. But the language was dead, lost, forgotten. Whatever those people stood for, bled for, argued over, desired and fought for…all those things were lost to the sand.

The father explained as best as he could:

"Early in its day, the most learned tribesmen of this place competed to create new ways of trading and production. But a sense of self-importance took over this branch, and other branches, of their kingdom.

"Over time, there was less and less innovation – and less communication with the other branches. There was a sense by this branch that they had mastered this environment, so they focused more on self-congratulation and worry (depending on the fruits of the season) than they did on fundamental customs and rituals. Creativity slowed, and paradoxically, so did its companion – compliance. After all, the tools and methods started to look dated, so less and less attention was paid to their upkeep.

"There were a few random surges of initiative. But once the people lost their way, those surges quickly ebbed. Tools became artifacts. This site became a museum instead of a commercial staging point. While it was still living, this place became a reliquary – a place to keep ancient artifacts. One day, no one could remember which of the artifacts were important…or why."

The father finished, "A few lucky people left the kingdom; many others starved while the few remaining leaders spent much of their time arguing over the meaning and purpose of various icons. These sands could not hear their arguments and did not care to hear them. The disagreeable members of the kingdom unwittingly conspired with the sand to wear away this once magnificent structure. The rhythm of trade here slowly died."

After a brief quiet, the daughter asked, "How do you know all this, father?"

He answered, "Lele, my father's mother's father was a branch manager for this tribe. I don't know what happened to him. But maybe there is something here for you to learn. From the extinct kingdom – and from this environment, which patiently waits for you to drop your guard – for you to stop caring and to stop thinking – and then it snatches away all that you cared and thought about."

Going Out on a Limb…

Just like the tribe in our previous example, no branch professional today plans to become extinct. After all, our branches are not reliquaries – places to keep ancient and mysterious artifacts – our branches today are active instruments of commerce. Places where discipline and new ideas combine to create an environment that attracts and retains great people.

<u>Or is that overstating the case for some of us</u>? Let's face facts...despite every company's assertions to the contrary, not every company has "the best people." If they really did, that distinction would be meaningless.

When everyone has the best, no one does. And just like customer service, just saying you're the best doesn't make it so. Who really believes you? Why?

Is your field network on the path to extinction? Or can you learn, like the wise man's daughter, from the lessons of your colleagues in other branch-based businesses? How can you use those lessons to drive continuous improvement in your field locations?

The fact is, we all face the same questions our ancestors did when they tried to roam, to trade, to colonize, to "branch out to more than one place" at the same time. Early nations seeking to control multiple locations from a central governing source took great risks (and usually paid a great price) to do so. Companies investing in multiple locations take a similar risk; and expect a correspondingly high return on investment.

Capital is risked in the belief that branches will repeatedly and consistently execute a proven method. Despite this belief, the conventional thinking in many branches is that "we are different." And there are differences. But successful branch leadership is increasingly impatient with offices that use their "difference" only as an excuse for slow or poor performance ("in our business...in our market..., etc."). When things are going well, the "market difference" isn't given the credit very often – so why should it shoulder all the blame?

If you have 500 offices today, you know it is impossible to manage 500 different initiatives for increasing profitability; your executive team is most effective when executing <u>repeatable methods</u> across the entire organization. We are defining a branch as an operating unit opened and supported by a remote corporate location. To the people in the branch, the <u>branch is not remote</u>. Corporate is remote. No judgment there, not good remote or bad remote – but corporate is geographically separated from the branch.

The First Branch Office

Ever since the first branch was opened...and Adam and Eve were put in charge, we've been trying to figure out how to make this branch idea work for us. But if we consider the allegory, "corporate" had a plan, Adam and Eve were put in place to execute it, they received some rules to follow (actually only one), and what happened? What was their response?

Well, being God's branch wasn't good enough for Adam and Eve. No, they didn't want to live in God's branch – they wanted to run their own corporate office! So they bit the apple and instead of having just one rule, God gave us ten rules. And considering the trouble we had with one rule, how are we now doing with the ten?

Despite its title, this is not just a book about field operations. This is a book about being successful in more than one place at once. About how we operate as human beings, about what makes us succeed and fail in certain small-group endeavors. Its content is highly relevant to branch operations; I use the branch to frame our expedition because I have experience in that milieu. Having worked with branches in 20 states and the District of Columbia, I've seen firsthand, like many readers, how people work together when given instructions from afar.

In studying the questions presented in this book, I personally interviewed individuals currently working in branch operations – or running them as executives in branch-based businesses. I'm not talking about a checklist survey, but in-depth interviews with people who share something in common – that thing that they share is that their career depends on branch performance. These individuals come from just about every industry – their candor and perspective makes this analysis possible.

I also am relying on the written input of over a dozen experts. None of them would be offended to have their expertise (and mine) characterized as a collection of experience based on mistakes made, seen and remedied. Their contribution to the book is immense. I am not an architect – so I rely on an architect to present design and site selection considerations. I am not a relocation expert – so I rely on a relocation expert to share successes and failures related to "branch migration." You, the reader, are the beneficiary of these and the other experts' observations.

Why does this book exist? Why was it written?

The better question is: why wasn't it written earlier?

There are countless books and strategies on vertical markets (concerns by industry) and functional areas (sales, marketing, management, accounting). But the branch, the store, the operating unit separated from the mother ship – these are neither fish nor fowl: they cross many vertical markets and all functional disciplines. According to In-Stat/MDR, there are over 3,500,000 remote site locations (although I would call them "sites with remote support"). They are emerging as a <u>diagonal market</u> with unique needs.

Earlier in my career, I opened a new office for a service company that had offices on five continents. Two years after opening that office, the team in my branch was recognized as having built the "Model Office" for the U.S. operations of that company. During and since that time, I have been intrigued with what makes certain offices great – and why so many branch operations struggle with the task before them.

If a company operates via branches, that company does so with its own set of unique expectations for its branches. But that same company also has universal expectations, expectations that are not unique – they are found across all industries and whenever instructions are given from afar:

- Local Reproduction (growth in same-store sales)
- Avoidance of a Wasteful Lifestyle (finding efficiencies and economies of scale)
- Follow the Rules (compliance with brand standards)

Shown visually, these goals can be seen to feed each other:

Whether we're talking about the world's first branch, your branch(es), or those of competitors, vendors, or customers, these are universal goals. We each have challenges unique to our situation, but the goals shown above are desired by all branches.

Why does the identification of this common ground matter? If you've ever assumed responsibility for a branch already in operation (not a startup), you know that one of the first things you will hear from the

Goals in the Field

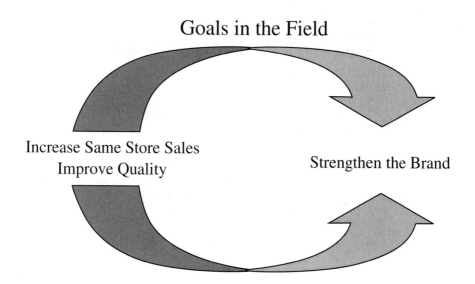

Increase Same Store Sales
Improve Quality

Strengthen the Brand

locals is, "We are different here." And they are. But why not start by finding just a few things in common?

For example, we're both interested in increasing sales, right? How about improving quality and strengthening the brand? OK, if all we can agree upon at first are those three items, we have the foundation for a great relationship. A relationship where the differences will be an asset rather than an excuse.

Organizationally, there can be huge differences in branch strategy. And there should be! One thing that makes each branch organization special and unique is the different answer it provides to the question:

"If we want to put inventory and decision-making closer to our customers, what is the best way for our company to do that?"

That is where the discussion leads to the number of offices, size of operations, franchise vs. company-owned, etc. Noticeably absent from this book are separate sections for the branches and for corporate. That's because whether you work in a well-run branch organization, or you work in a disastrously mismanaged branch organization, corporate and the branches cannot be separated. Corporate and the branches are different parts of the same body.

The goal of every branch should be to create, test and execute improvements within its organization. Branches should avoid wanting to "be corporate," that is to take over corporate; instead they should strive to model the behavior that will show their organization what is possible in the field.

By the same measure, the goal of every corporate office should be to promote "field" success, not to promote "corporate office" success. It is a plain fact that, while some branches can succeed despite poor corporate support, no corporate can succeed independently of its branches. Who cares how great your HR platform is, how advanced your help-desk is, or how smart corporate marketing is...if those things don't lead to performance improvements and profitability in the branches!

Who cares within a vacuum? Nobody. On the other hand, when those corporate functions give the branches a competitive edge, they become a key part of how the company differentiates itself.

Requiem for a Branch: Who Died There?

What makes or breaks an individual branch? What determines whether that field operation lives or dies?

The people working there. And the method by which they execute for their customers.

The # 1 expense in almost all branch organizations is personnel expense. But the return on investment varies greatly by person. Even within the same company: if you think about the difference in productivity between your best employee and your worst employee today, can that difference be explained solely by whether they work in a best or worst location? No. If that were the case, there would never be a need to measure individual performance.

Interviews with branch professionals revealed many challenges and they are discussed in some detail in the next chapter. One area, though, deserves its own place in the sun: the characters we work with day-in and day-out in the intimacy of the branch setting.

Say you're part of an organization with 10,000 employees, but each day you work with a team of 12 in your local branch. What's the source of most of your energy or frustration? Good or bad, it's often the 12 people you work with directly. It's the manager who leads by example. It's the sales rep who is so disconnected from operations that you don't know whether to root for more business or not. It's the Director of First Impressions who answers the phone. These are the folks that give you fuel or sap your strength. But you're not the center of the universe - what's their impression of you?

Instead of focusing on one industry or one part of the country, let's journey away from the business world and visit a rain forest. Once we're there, we'll note what type of personalities we observe. We'll use the rain forest as our starting point because, just like in many field offices, the residents are interested primarily in their own survival...and they express that interest in myriad ways.

Mobile Monkey – a survivor, he or she hops from one branch to another; sometimes within the same tree (your company), sometimes from tree-to-tree (among competitors).

Turf Monkey – "Boogala, boogala, this is my turf! Stay away from my location!! I don't need to waste my time with monkeys from other branches. Why don't you leave me alone and let me run my monkey business???"

Traitor Monkey – he or she puts personal popularity above the mission of the brand. "Don't listen to those gorillas from corporate. I'm the Man around here." This perspective is usually promoted both to employees and customers. "Looks like I'm going to have to clean up after corporate again..."

Savage Monkey – "Aaarrgghh – the sky is falling, can't you see I'm busy! We've got another crisis!!!! Can't you idiots do anything right? Do I have to beat you with my monkey stick? Get out of my way!"

Sniper Monkey – "This branch is a great place to shoot at other monkeys...monkeys at corporate, monkeys in other branches, even monkeys in my own branch! Look at that monkey over there – he doesn't work as hard as I do. I don't think Suzy Simian is carrying her weight, do you?"

Rule Monkey – "According to section 3.2a, we have to copy these in triplicate. I'll bet if I spend three hours locked in my 'branch' office I can figure out a way to chart these rules in Excel. Yippee!" This monkey tries to comply with each rule, but refuses to use his or her vision to seek the greater goal.

Dreamer Monkey – this is the innovator whose ideas never go anywhere because they are never shared or consistently executed. The Dreamer Monkey views Utopia as an excuse rather than a destination..."If these idiots around here would only listen to my brilliant ideas..."

Slumlord Monkey – handed a perfectly good branch, this slob lets it slowly go to seed.

Puffed Up Monkey – "Whatever is important in this branch setting, well I mastered it long ago. Look at me. I'm important and the rest of you are not. It's obvious by your lack of taste in monkey finery."

Puffed Up Monkey "Professionals"– articulated with a fake Brahmin accent: "Our firm is better than your firm. We are monkey professionals. We don't talk about things like branch or store management...our service and intellect is self-evident. We are smarter than everyone else in the forest, including our clients. Especially our clients. Here is my invoice for the time it took to conduct this discussion."

Greedy Monkey – "The branch is my personal piggy bank. As long as I'm making money, why rock the boat? Why should I care that other branches and corporate trust me to deliver?"

Lamprey Monkey – this branch-dweller shares DNA with the ancient lamprey, a prehistoric fish that would attach its considerable teeth to a host and then parasitically suck sustenance from the host. In a business field operation, this character sucks the life out of the same old accounts...its lifespan as a parasite is dependent solely on how long its host (account) lives.

Innocent Monkey – these are the new branch denizens. They are trusting and open to new ideas. In their earliest days, they often see opportunities related to process and quality that grow less obvious with time. If you want to know what your branch looks like to the visiting customer, the Innocent Monkey has the closest perspective.

Scavenger Monkey – "Look a piece of half-rotten fruit dropped from that branch. I guess I can eat today. I really don't feel like fishing or cooking or cleaning. Let's see what floats to the surface of the pond today and eat it. Tomorrow, after the worker monkeys are done picking over the remains of that dead goat, I'm gonna have me a nice piece of sun-dried jungle meat. Hope there's something left – yum!"

Diligent Monkey – Gather the food. Build a shelter to protect the other monkeys. Observe and encourage. Develop new tools. Reproduce responsibly...

Of course, these are merely hypothetical creatures. We don't have Turf Monkeys or Puffed Up Monkeys in our branches, do we? Here's how to use our friends from the rain forest: the next time you meet a Scavenger Monkey in one of your branches, don't get mad, just quietly smile and think of him or her in this other-worldly context. Remember that he or she would rather eat roadkill than listen to you talk about brand standards – so go find a Diligent Monkey to work with instead!

Let's return from this weird world of the rain forest and spend some time with people working in branch operations today. We're going to share the comments of real-world branch professionals from many parts of the world. To get started, let's consider the journey of one man as he built a career – going from the role of Branch Manager in Memphis, TN to being the President of that multi-billion dollar company to serving as an entrepreneur in an emerging field.

Chapter Two:
From Branch Manager to President - Lessons Learned

FT: When you think back on your career, and the different positions you held within branch-based businesses, what would you say is unique about "growing up" in a branch environment?

RP: Frank, I've never had a job that wasn't in a branch organization. I think the biggest advantage to having a career in that type of environment is the visibility. What I mean by that is there is an opportunity to be seen – by your peers, by customers, by your corporate team. It's not like you are just one of 5,000 people showing up to work on a giant corporate campus. Each branch is a fishbowl, which can be a huge advantage if you work hard and deliver results.

This chapter was written in cooperation with Richard A. Piske III.

Mr. Piske is a Senior Managing Director with Kelly Services, Inc. He is a co-founder of Kelly FedSecure and 3PR Corporation. He was once a Branch Manager – for the Memphis branch of Olsten Corporation – and took on additional responsibilities over a 17-year career there, finishing as the President of U.S. commercial staffing operations, with responsibility for $2 Billion in revenue. I interviewed him to get his perspective on the journey from Branch Manager to President.

Mr. Piske serves as a founding member of the Branch Productivity Institute's BPI Congress.

FT: Let's go back in time a bit. Back before the executive responsibilities and the authority that goes along with them. Back to the time when you were a Branch Manager – one of hundreds in your company. What made you successful as a Branch Manager?

RP: What worked for me - and what I would tell the Branch Manager reading your book is, "Act like it is your business, because it is." My peer group didn't always act that way, and it got their branches into trouble.

FT: When you say, "Act like it is your business," what do you mean by that?

RP: It's all about caring, not because someone is watching, but because you care. There are a few areas where I can give you some examples: expenses, customer service, and hiring. OK, relative to expenses, I've seen people that wouldn't spend a nickel of their own money for a shoeshine, but they'd order that extra drink at dinner because they think, "it's just the company's money." Folks who put their family up at a Holiday Inn when they're on vacation but want to stay at the Four Seasons when it's on the company's dime. Managers who keep a poorly performing employee on the payroll for an extra month or so. Things they would never do if they acted like it was their own business.

FT: What about customer service? How does that relate to acting like it is your business?

RP: My motto has always been "Never be Large Enough to Afford the Loss of a Single Customer." A bylaw of that motto is that, as the branch manager, you handle every problem personally. I never delegated a problem - as a Branch Manager, I couldn't afford to. And when your people see you handling the tough issues, they respect you. Another area in customer service is that the Branch Manager sets the pace.

What I mean by that is, whatever you do, they will follow. My first office opened for business at 7:30 a.m. each day. I started coming in around 7:00, just so I could get a jump on the day - you know how you can get things done when it's quiet. Well it wasn't long before my people starting coming in closer to 7:00 a.m. as well! Which was great, and it meant I had to start coming in before 7:00 to get some work done before the day started. Now if I didn't care about the business and came in a half hour later than my people, because I was "the boss," that would have sent a terrible message and it would have been less effective.

FT: You mentioned hiring. How did hiring relate to your practice of acting like it was your business?

RP: Hire the best. That's it. Your gut is never wrong – don't go against your instincts just because you have an open slot to fill. Don't hire the best of the worst. Hire the best. Hire people that are better than you are. It takes longer, but in my case it was worth it and it was substantiated by no turnover.

FT: How did your peers at the time describe you?

RP: Competitive. Knowledgeable. Threatening. A Source of Best Practices. Approachable.

FT: How were you threatening and approachable at the same time?

RP: What I mean by threatening is that they knew I was highly competitive and my branch was gunning for the top spot. If their branch was in the top spot and mine wasn't there yet, they knew my branch was going to be a serious threat to their position. But I shared ideas and I asked for help – so I was approachable too.

Within your branch, you have to stay close to the people. If you touch the people, you'll never get surprised. Read their emotions and accommodate their occasional personal crises.

FT: What does "Competitive" mean to you?

RP: I firmly believe you have to have arch-rivals to get your blood going. You know the emotional intensity that's generated by a homecoming game? I targeted a couple competitors and told my people – it is unacceptable to lose against these two companies. And we picked the best competitors as targets. And we beat them because we cared intensely, emotionally, about beating those targets. When those competitors were no longer the best, when we surpassed their performance, we picked someone else to target locally.

FT: You said your peers would describe you as knowledgeable. What type of knowledge are you talking about?

RP: I knew my business and I knew my market. I'll tell you a story. As a new Branch Manager, I inherited two experienced salespeople and one of them had a "what do you know" attitude about working with me as the new manager. Well, I wasn't offended or hurt by that. I knew that to earn their respect, I had to be better than the best salesperson – more innovative, more creative.

You have to know the job you are asking someone else to do. Otherwise, how can you help them do it better? And you have to know more about your market than anyone else. This is a real common weakness: poor intel. But everybody thinks they are good at it, don't they? Most aren't.

FT: Tell me about why you were promoted.

RP: Two reasons. I always had the best people. And I always had the best financial performance. One leads to the other – and you have to have both.

FT: Let's talk about this idea of "best people." What does that mean?

RP: It's about recruiting and retention. A good Branch Manager is always recruiting. I don't mean run an ad every week, but network; ask for referrals. I remember one time I was struggling to find excellent salespeople – remember I don't just hire the best of the worst. So I looked beyond my industry, the staffing industry, and asked myself, "What other companies are like staffing companies?" I targeted a couple of parallel industries and set myself up as a John Doe in a friend's office. I then called target companies and said, "I need to talk to your best salesperson." When they called on me, I decided whether they met my expectations and I hired some excellent people that way. That process also told the salespeople something about my competitive nature.

I can't tell you how many times I saw a manager accept mediocrity. They weren't as thorough. Every resume tells a story – and you need to make sure there are no missing chapters on the resume sitting in front of you. A $50,000 salary is a $250,000 - $500,000 decision – so you need to treat it like that.

FT: What else can you tell us about recruiting?

RP: You are looking for people that are better and smarter than you are. People that are challengers. People who will do something for you – you know, in our industry you wanted people that would act and then ask for forgiveness later, rather than someone who couldn't make a move without your permission.

You empower people like that.

FT: What about financial performance as one of the criteria for promotion?

RP: Yes, it's important – you have to have it. But it is not enough just to have solid financial performance. Because you promote a person, not a market. Maybe it's just a good market they are working in.

FT: So what was the balance between the factors of (1) hiring great people and (2) financially performing?

RP: When promoting a Branch Manager to the next level, you intend to make a change in the way the organization looks. The hiring and retention is really what you are promoting – the financial performance is just the proof that the Branch Manager is good at hiring and retention.

What I had – and what I wanted in the people I promoted – was the ability to balance the competing ideas of "don't micromanage" and "pay a lot of attention to detail."

FT: How do you manage all the details without micromanaging?

RP: You start by realizing that management is the art of getting someone to do something. I didn't tell people "do this, do that" but I had 10,000 questions about what we were doing and how we were doing it. People don't like saying "I don't know" so once you've asked them a certain question a few times, they work hard to always know the answer.

FT: How does the job of President differ from that of Branch Manager?

RP: As a Branch Manager, I had to know what to do and I had to do it.

As the President, you have to know how to make other people do what needs to be done. You lead them by example, but you don't do it for them.

As President, you've got to be much more strategic and less focused on tactical issues. By strategic I mean you have to be able to look way out in front of the airplane: where are the opportunities and hazards? What's the shelf life of our current products? If you have to focus on tactical issues as President, you are in trouble.

FT: What do you mean by tactical issues?

RP: Number of sales calls, pipeline, accounts receivable. These things are hugely important, but you need to have good people focused on those areas, and then you can work on coaching your management team to improve against metrics – but if you are the President of a branch-based organization and you are personally counting sales calls each week, you have a problem.

FT: Where did you learn about tactics and strategy?

RP: For me, it was mostly internal vs. external sources. When you are a Branch Manager, you have to be tactically sound and you learn that mostly from internal sources. You do what I did...you fall into some holes, make mistakes, learn. I was completely self-taught – my supervisor was 1500 miles away. You use your instincts and judgment – you learn. Very few companies have the right training infrastructure in place to accelerate that learning – but when they do, it's a huge advantage for them.

When you are in the executive suite, you still learn internally, but you also use a lot more external resources. I read a lot. I learn from customers. I learn from our best vendors – I learned a lot and improved our financial performance with ideas from USI and Rosenbluth, for example.

FT: You said that you read a lot. How did your reading list change as you made the journey from Branch Manager to President?

RP: Well, it did change. As a Branch Manager, I read the local business journal, the local newspapers. I read about chamber events and things that impacted my local prospects. As a President, I read Fortune, Forbes, Newsweek, the Wall Street Journal, Time. I read industry information from the American Staffing Association and Staffing Industry Analysts.

FT: What elements in the two jobs are the same?

RP: You must hire great people. You must retain them. Regardless of the outside environment, you must do better than the competition. It's so easy to say, "We fell back 10% or we grew 10%." But how did the competitor do in that same period? In both positions, you have to have an insatiable quest to win.

FT: Did you know you would become President when you were a Branch Manager?

RP: I never thought when I was a Branch Manager that I would be President. I joined the company because it was a great opportunity. The company had integrity, which is non-negotiable with me. I liked the operating style and culture – and these things are hugely important, they will trump any personal characteristics.

FT: What do you mean by that?

RP: You put the best person into a horrible or unethical environment, they will not succeed. It would be like running Secretariat at the bottom of a gravel pit. You have to find a company whose operating style and culture fits your own.

FT: Any other thoughts on the two positions of Branch Manager and President?

RP: <u>Just that the future Presidents of the Fortune 500 are probably working as Branch Managers today.</u>

FT: What did you worry about as a Branch Manager that, in hindsight, was not worth worrying about?

RP: That's a tough question because I believe many Branch Managers don't worry enough.

But to answer your question, maybe it's worrying what other people think. No, not even that. I've seen field staff tangle with corporate support people just because they can. It's not a good move. All in all, I'd say if you are Branch Manager, you get paid to worry, so you should be thinking about possible threats and opportunities all the time – it's just the nature of the job and doing it well.

FT: If you knew then what you know now, what would you have done differently as a Branch Manager?

RP: The workplace has changed dramatically in the past 20 years. I think it is much more important today to cultivate mentoring relationships at multiple levels. You just don't know how long a single mentor will be in a position to guide you, especially if that mentor is also your boss. I also think it is easier to learn from other organizations today, to benchmark practices with people outside of your own organization.

FT: How has the job of Branch Manager changed during the past 20 years?

RP: There's about a half dozen major changes that come to mind.

1. You must be very good at marketing today. It is critical today to have a strong knowledge of your competition, and also to understand finance.

2. Today, you have to be better at creating and continuously changing value for the customer. Product lifecycles are shorter, so you've got to constantly innovate if you want to preserve or grow margins.

3. The intensity is more acute. Among selling Branch Managers, the difference between "the best and the rest" is going to continue to become more pronounced. Customers are more jealous of their time and their information, so the level of business acumen that was acceptable years ago will not suffice today and going forward.

4. You have to move more quickly and thoroughly on human resources problems.

5. Automation has made a big difference for some companies. It changes where you put your branches, and how many you need, but it only makes a difference if it addresses your key success factors. There are plenty of poorly run operations that are automated. And plenty of companies who have written checks for tens of millions of dollars worth of hardware/software and they've just automated a business premise that was weak to begin with.

6. I think employees are more demanding; they are more litigious and work/life balance seems to be more important.

FT: What surprised you once you hit the executive suite?

RP: In a former company, I was amazed at the way decisions were made. The lack of knowledge in some quarters about the guts of the business. The politics. You have to hold onto your ethics and high standards, because in the end that's your currency. Political gains are short-lived.

FT: What do you mean by that?

RP: The political ebbs and flows are much more severe, and much shorter-term, than the business ebbs and flows. They don't always follow logic and reason and you have to be prepared for that.

FT: As the President, what did you want every Branch Manager working for you to know?

RP: Number One is knowing the competition. You cannot know too much. You need to know how they think, their values, their strengths and weaknesses, even who they are hiring.

Know your customers. We won a contract in my Memphis branch, got the contract signed, before the competition even knew the customer was moving to town.

You also need to understand the financial levers in your branch. The incremental ways that your branch makes or loses money. I noticed a real training need in this area.

FT: Why do you use the competition as your first crucible, instead of the customers?

RP: I know this is counter-intuitive, because the customer is what puts bread on the table. But in the end, the customer is not just looking for a product or a relationship - they are looking for the best product and relationship. The word "best" in this context suggests there are alternatives for the customer – and your branch must beat those alternatives.

When I hear people say, "Don't focus too much on the competition," I ask, "Who did you lose your last ten deals to?" It's always the same answer: the competition. So you have to understand the strengths and weaknesses of the other team: they are whom you are taking the field against.

I guess a final point is in order here, Frank. I never said, "It's the only thing to focus on." I just said it's the first. How you stack up against your competitors tests how your customers perceive your value in the real world – customers vote for a winner with their dollars, so you better know your opponent.

FT: What else?

RP: Know that your gut is never wrong. That for better or for worse, people do not change. So hire for values; look for competitive instinct.

FT: OK, so that is what you wanted every Branch Manager to know. What did you want every Branch Manager to do?

RP: Make decisions – do something. A great way to test this is to ask them every week, "What is the most important decision you made for your branch this week?"

Have client visibility – personal, intimate relationships with the top customer group. The fact is – nothing happens in the office; you cannot spend too much time with customers.

Be energetic – name some rivals to your branch; break down the silos and talk to people in other branches.

FT: What happens when you follow these rules?

RP: Well it took me from Memphis to New York. From being the Branch Manager to being the President. And it has worked for people that worked for me, as well. Seven of my direct reports have gone on to a position of President of their organization.

FT: Any other advice for the Branch Manager reading this book?

RP: Being a leader means being out in front. Not just physically (working in the trenches, which you have to do). But mentally as well. Your team wants to hear your vision for the business, and why your business deserves to be its market leader.

I've worked with you on this book because I care about the subject matter. I want to make "the branch" a better place to work. If a person understands and adopts the principles in Branching Out, it could define their personal legacy within their company or industry - and result in a million dollars or more of additional earnings over the remainder of their career.

Chapter Three:

Vices & Sin...That Will Do Your Branches In

If your organization opens field operations seeking greater, local customer intimacy in its local markets, what gets in the way of that worthy goal? What vices[2] prevent branch virtuosity? We asked those questions and here's what we heard.

Candid interviews with field managers and executives within branch-based organizations revealed some real barriers to branch success in their companies. People that work in branches every day are not blind to what works and what hurts – they felt these issues most affected the branches in their organization.

We'll list some of them first, and then work on organizing them...

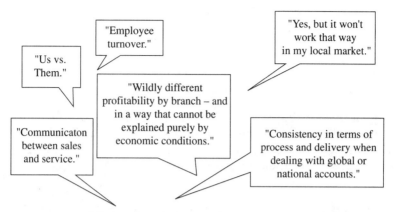

"Us vs. Them."

"Employee turnover."

"Yes, but it won't work that way in my local market."

"Communicaton between sales and service."

"Wildly different profitability by branch – and in a way that cannot be explained purely by economic conditions."

"Consistency in terms of process and delivery when dealing with global or national accounts."

...Plus numerous additional variations on one issue...communications!

This is just a sample of some of the different issues people indicated were affecting their branch organization's performance. I'm not personally interested in problems for their own sake. Instead, I wanted to examine these distractions in the context of whether they affected branch morale and local brand achievements. As important, I wanted to see how the problems were connected – whether there was a pattern to their cause and effect. Considering this challenge, we grouped the responses into 15 different categories as a starting point for mapping the problems.

Some of these 15 "Barriers to Branch Success" may appear in your organization: left unchecked they are a drag on those universal goals for branch businesses: increasing same-store sales, reducing inefficiencies and building a stronger brand

As you consider these obstacles, consider whether the barrier being described is present in your organization – and what evidence exists to support that conclusion.

Vice # 1: Noncompliance with Brand Standards

Simply stated, this is where the only thing remote branches have in common is the brand on the door – and even that may have mutated into different versions.

Some examples of this barrier include:

• Recent, or incomplete, integration of multiple companies under one brand.
• Failure to perform key operational tasks in a brand-consistent manner.
• Failure to address national account concerns consistently.
• Extreme differences in hiring process and criteria from branch-to-branch.

- Lack of brand standards; where each office is seen as more of an outpost connected to its industry than standing for anything unique to its brand.
- Public compliance, private defiance.

Vice # 2: Wrong Things Centralized

The branch operating model is either (a) the most cost-effective way to get resources closer to the customers or (b) the most costly and inefficient way to operate. The difference in these two outcomes is the difference between mere footprint and market leadership.

Think about it. If a company needs 500 employees to reach its current goals, is it cheaper or more expensive to have all 500 located under one roof – or under 30 roofs? Is it easier to control the management of one location or of 30 locations? Is it easier to adopt a compensation and benefit plan that meets the regulatory hurdles of one jurisdiction – or of 30? From the get-go, and from every angle, geographically diversifying the workforce is more expensive.

So why do companies opt for the branch model? Some shouldn't. But for those organizations that want (or need) to get resources closer to the customers, a well-run branch structure is highly competitive. The key to getting resources closer to customers in a cost-effective manner: improve organizational decision-making, one facet of which is <u>getting decision-making closer to the customer.</u>

Does this mean corporate should abdicate all responsibility to the field and hope for the best based on geographic proximity? No. The simple fact is that some branches know less about their customers from a mile away than their corporate knows from 1500 miles away. How is this possible? Because every local office does not always operate at peak sales efficiency.

Some examples of this barrier include:

- Local offices making long-term decisions (for only their office) about site selection, "special" compensation plans, marketing campaigns, sales process.
- Introducing centralized bureaucratic hoops into the hiring process, instead of developing consistent hiring criteria and process – and letting the field run with it.
- People without accountability for revenue getting overly involved in account strategy.
- People without accountability for delivery developing business processes to test on the field (also known as the development of a self-perceived genius class within corporate).

Think about the types of decisions you want to place closer to the customers and see if these distinctions make sense:

- Decentralize the ability to respond to customer problems. Centralize the recording and measurement of customer problems.
- Decentralize short-term decision-making. Centralize long-term decision-making (with input from local offices).
- Decentralize hiring and promotion. Centralize the formation of hiring and retention planning (including rewards programs).
- Decentralize individual account-planning. Centralize the creation and review of an account planning process.
- Decentralize competitive intelligence gathering. Centralize the analysis of that activity.

Vice # 3: Unfocused Sales Activity

First, who is your customer?

Second, what do you have that they want?

Third, the last time your customer switched suppliers, why did they do that?

Can you articulate the answers to those three questions?

If the answer is yes to the articulation question, you know whom to target, why and how. Once that understanding is accepted as valid, the required sales activity either happens or it doesn't. If the required sales activity is communicated and it does not happen, you've got a huge red flag.

Here's what it looks like:

- Selling to the wrong types of customer, thus wasting time and resources on dead-ends.
- Using a message that does not make it easier for customers to buy (for example, lacking differentiators or boring your prospects).
- Using a process that does not make it easier for customers to buy (for example, confusing the customer at the point of purchase).
- Failing to meet the sales activity standards established by the company (for example in a B2B setting, meeting with six customers per week when ten is required).
- Lack of follow-up (for example, lots of intro calls, no depth in the pipeline).
- Monotonous follow-up (for example, no new account penetration, just baby-sitting customers where the same questions get asked every week, 52 times/year – "Hey, how 'bout dem Redwings?").

Vice # 4: Stale Product; Reduced Lifecycle

Big danger here. And one to which branch organizations are particularly susceptible: commoditization.

The fact that a footprint of many branches is required in your business means that there are needs for customer intimacy in many places – all at the same time.

As your product or service ages, as competitors seek to duplicate your service methods, your product or services gets commoditized and the need for a local presence diminishes. (I didn't say, "Goes away.") This happens at precisely the same time that your investments in those local operations are increasing. This is the rainbow[3] of life & death.

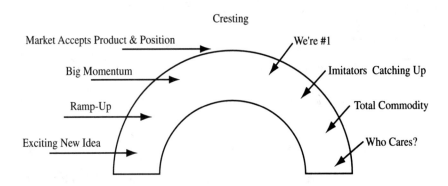

It represents part of the life cycle for a branch organization. One negative outcome of this life cycle is a funeral for your business - or at least for many of your branches. There are two complementary and positive strategies for reincarnation under this life cycle. They are (1) greater sales efficiency and operational efficiency (competition and victory on a pure commodity basis) and (2) innovation in the form of new products and services (use the commodity as a platform from which to develop new products).

There is nothing wrong with either positive strategy – together they are a powerful way to extend the lifecycle of your branch and your business. Alone, the first approach looks like efficiency without innovation – which means you will be competing on price. The second invests reliable cash flow from your commodity to fund new, higher margin products and services – but it only works if you keep that cash flowing: innovation without brand discipline supporting it creates only short-lived advantages.

Some indications of the "stale product" barrier include:

• Commodity businesses that seek regulatory protection.
• Lack of enthusiasm by sales force and customers.

- Mature vertical markets that are unprofitable or marginally profitable (seeking "last-man standing" status).
- Businesses that make a lot of noise about "quality" or "service" <u>where no one outside the company believes them</u>.
- In a sales call, the salesperson differentiates only by saying, "The difference is me" and cannot point to a single (believable) organizational advantage.
- Where Travel & Entertainment Expense significantly outweighs Research & Development Expense.
- Businesses with no new products or services!
- Too much golf. Wow, can there be too much golf? Well, to risk offending some of the readership, ask how much long-term value was created by the 400 rounds of golf played with customers last year. No moral judgment here: in a commodity business, maybe golf is important and one's handicap might be a legitimate piece of the hiring criteria…if you are in a commoditized business and you expect it to stay that way. But that means your customers are buying golf instead of your product or service.

What have you done lately? How is your relationship from the customer different from ten years ago? When local people talk only about the "relationship" being key, this is usually an indication that the company has not created anything new. And the local office usually places a much higher premium on the "relationship" than the customer does.

While the word "relationship" means something important to all companies, it rises to the level of a sacred cow in declining companies: a word that everyone nods to in solemn agreement. But what does it mean? It reminds me of the old saw, "Marriage is a great institution, but who wants to be institutionalized?" You marry for love, not "to be married." Customers buy because they have a need – don't fool yourself into thinking that their greatest need is just the "relationship." No one is that likeable!

Put another way, it's nice to have clients that are also friends – but they wouldn't be your friends for long if you weren't performing. The performance matters more than the relationship.

Vice # 5: Lamprey Lifestyle

A lamprey is an aquatic vertebrate with prehistoric origins. As discussed earlier, it has a jawless mouth with a set of strong teeth. The lamprey parasitically attaches itself to its host and sucks and sucks and sucks. It's an uninvited guest that stays too long.

A lamprey branch is one that continues to milk existing relationships without adding anything new to the mix. No new accounts. No new ideas. Just sucking away, holding on for dear life in the hope that the host never dries up and dies. What a way to live!

Some examples of this barrier include:

• No new account activity.
• No best practices reported and shared.
• No competitive analysis performed – after all, "We're the best at relationship-building, we don't need to worry about the competitors!"
• Highly defensive regarding change.
• Can blindly live off the host until the host is dead – and then not even notice until someone tells them.
• Have forgotten how good it feels to open new accounts.

Vice # 6: Competitors React Faster to New Opportunities

When decision-making takes place too far from the customer, this is what happens. The competitor with strong brand guidelines coupled with local authority can always make a decision quicker – or get information faster – than someone who has to play long distance "hot potato." Some politically charged organizations are so good at discouraging local decision-making that they make the game of "hot potato" look more like bobbing for tater tots in the deep fryer.

Symptoms of this problem include:

• No one can seem to answer the question, "What is the most important decision you made for your branch this week? This year...?"
• Consistently losing "good people" to competitors during the hiring process.
• Prospects and customers believe (rightly or not) that your competition has invented most of the best practices in the market and everyone else is just playing catch-up.
• The competition just seems smarter – even their mistakes tend to pay off eventually.

Vice # 7: Tribal Negotiation

Oogah, oogah. Don't tell corporate anything. Sandbag on your budgets. What's good for us is...good for us. To hell with the company. That other office is a bunch of idiots. We are the smartest, best looking, hardest working people in the company. The further people are away from us, the uglier, dumber and lazier they are. If you want something from me, you always have to pay me homage first.

Does any of the following look familiar?

- First of all, every discussion is a negotiation.
- No cross-selling.
- High level of distrust among offices; even higher level of distrust among regions (but it's more polite…maybe).
- Eat or be eaten.
- High level of turnover among accounts and employees.
- No interest in supporting national account commitments, ever, no matter what, never.

Vice # 8: Opacity

Opacity defined: <u>impervious to the rays of light; unintelligible; hard to understand or explain</u>. From an outsider's perspective (corporate, another branch, a customer), what is going on past the walls inside these offices? Did you invest in 800 branch offices merely to wonder what was happening in 800 places – and to struggle mightily for the picture? No.

Some examples of opacity:

- Reluctance to host visitors from other branches or corporate ("We're too busy for those people in our company!")
- Unwillingness to invite customers to the office.
- Recalcitrance in providing operational feedback.
- Usually accompanied by an expectation of complete autonomy in local budgeting ("Just give us the money, we know what we're doing.").

Vice # 9: Drag Locations

The office that never makes money. Forget about demographic studies up-front, this one is located near the former manager's home, and (poorly) designed by his or her domestic partner. Not up to code as far as the brand look is concerned. Not a place that makes it easy for customers to do business with you. Not a place you are proud to recruit from. You know it when you see it:

- Above-market rental rates and time commitment.
- Below-market utility.
- "Bad feel."
- Poor proximity to customer needs.
- Poorly adapted to employee needs.
- You get a "victim tag" the minute you start working there – "this location is no good, we're gonna move in 18 months…"

Vice # 10: Culture Gap between Field and Corporate

Culture comes from the Latin root *cultura*, and shares that root with the word "cultivate." Are we all *growing* in the same direction? Are we cultivating things that are important to each other – that will last beyond this week or month?

When people say there is a culture gap between corporate and the field, I like to ask, "What part of corporate?" Corporate just looks like one big place to the field office because, well, it's one big place. But "corporate" is not monolithic. There are varying degrees of thought within corporate – just like there are within branches. That said, let's not argue with the underlying premise – when people feel like it's "us vs. them," there is a problem.

<u>The root of this problem, surprisingly, is not paranoia; it is "overconfidence":</u>

• "We are so smart, good-looking, etc. that the only people who can beat us are within our own organization."
• Whether at corporate or in the field, an inability to see that the real "us vs. them" is the competitor stealing your accounts.
• Over-reliance on charisma and political maneuvering.
• Belief by the corporate office that any problem can be solved with a new report or metric.
• Belief by the branch office that no problem can be solved through remote measurement and analysis.
• Condescension on either side.

Vice # 11: Not Enough Cross-Selling (Company History Buried)

The greatest irony in branch businesses: where your multiple locations fail to service the multiple locations of your existing prospects and customers. Also known as "having a footprint and not using it." Why does it happen? Often because branches want to make their own way in the world, without the burden of having to leverage other branches' success.

I personally remember hearing about a sales call in Texas where the branch manager didn't know (until it was pointed out as a "coincidence") that the person he was calling on was already a customer. The customer had relocated from a place where he had used our service through a different branch! Ouch!

Some working examples of this barrier include:

• No one assigned to monitor penetration in key accounts by product and location.
• It's left completely up to the branch to decide whom to call on – and who to service.

- Cross-selling is defined by these companies as "making more sales calls to the same companies so we can sell them more products in more locations." Noticeable absent is any strategy addressing why the customer would want to buy from you in multiple locations – and through fewer sales calls!
- No "company history calendar" showing key events in major accounts across all locations.

Vice # 12: Surprises in Branch Forecasting

Companies miss earnings estimates, and suffer the consequences, when they cannot accurately forecast results. Concomitantly, results cannot be forecast when activity cannot be accurately predicted. The root of this issue lies in local forecasting. There is an old saying that "guessing is cheap, guessing wrong is expensive" – and that adage surely applies to the failure to meet investor expectations.

It's safe to say that no organization opens myriad locations simply to reduce the likelihood of poor forecasting. In fact, weak methods in this area serve to compound the error rather than to reduce it. These surprises are rooted in a lack of trust – the field does not trust corporate enough to tell the truth. Corporate does not trust the field to meet expectations and creates a culture of non-accountability. What do these surprises look like?

- Revenue promises broken.
- "Necessary" expenses that were not planned for.
- Price reductions that were not anticipated or bargained for.
- Lost accounts with little notice.
- Unexpected abandonment of mission by key players.

Vice # 13: Best Practices Hidden or Silo'd

Earlier, I interviewed a gentleman who started his career as a branch manager and went on to run a multi-billion dollar company as the president. He asked a question that does a wonderful job of explaining why best practices are often trapped within silos of the organization...

"When was the last time you remember one sibling doing something with the intent of helping another sibling, or making that other sibling look good in the eyes of the parent(s)?"

In this question, we glimpse the cause behind the wasteful practice of hiding best practices. And we may see that since we can't expect the sharing of best practices to happen naturally, the role of organizational leadership is to facilitate its occurrence.

Some examples of silo'd best practices include:

- Not sharing information on account pursuit (see the related topic: inadequate cross-selling).
- Finding out that something works – and is important – and using that knowledge to "beat the other branches" instead of beating the other branches' competition.
- Not asking for help when you need it because you are afraid that request is a sign of weakness.
- Not revealing a model or prototype office.
- Worshipping results instead of activity coupled with results.

Vice # 14: Low Employee Morale/High Turnover

How much does it cost when your best people walk out the door? When your worst people slow down their productivity even further? Interviews with branch professionals revealed that this challenge is usually tied to process, communication and respect. By process, we mean the hiring process, the decision-making process, and the methods introduced to serve customers.

It is easy to forget that our <u>field office personnel get feedback constantly from their market</u> – at a frequency hundreds of times greater than the feedback they get from corporate or from other branches. This is a communication frequency gap...and to some extent it is healthy. After all, would you rather your branches ask corporate or customers ten times a day how they are doing? So the gap is OK. But corporate has to compensate for the gap by providing a vision.

When the local feedback so outweighs the brand vision, morale declines and the branches go native.

The good news: declines in morale are rarely if ever permanent for an employee. The bad news: the reason those declines are temporary is that the employee will seek a better environment elsewhere once they hit their breaking point.

Some common warning signs:

- Us vs. Them is focused internally.
- Slow growth or no growth.
- Increase in expenses relative to revenues produced.
- Culture of disposability: long-term use of the same management sticks instead of a carrot and stick balance.
- Rude or sharp language between peers.
- The idea of getting fired becomes exciting and liberating!
- Field turnover far exceeds corporate turnover.

Vice # 15: Technology and Process Gaps

The system doesn't work – it's cumbersome. Or there is no system. The processes in the company seem more oriented toward risk reduction and measurement than cultivation and development.

Some examples of these gaps include:

• Cost reduction without gain-sharing (either with employees or customers).
• Systems that reduce the number of decision-opportunities.
• Redundant data entry requirements.
• The training connection between the new system and customer values is tangential at best.
• Significant time spent doing things that do not contribute to the "magic moments" in the organization.
• Automation that reduces the opportunity for innovation instead of increasing it.
• The people proposing the system (the corporate genius class or the vendor genius class) actively pretend to understand your customer's requirements without asking for your field's input.

OK, we made it. Fifteen barriers. Fifteen obstacles to greater profitability. Fifteen issues that, unaddressed, increase isolation and reduce brand strength. In the next chapter, we will organize these issues into a format categorizing them by cause and effect, and by whether corporate or the field can most immediately effectuate change.

Chapter Four:
Sorting Out the Problems & Finding the Model

Noncompliance with Brand Standards	Wrong Things Centralized	Unfocused Sales Activity	Stale Product: Reduced Lifecycle	Lamprey Lifestyle
Competitors React Faster to New Opportunities	Tribal Negotiation	Opacity	Drag Locations	Culture Gap between Field & Corporate
Not Enough Cross-Selling (Company History Buried)	Surprises In Branch Forecasting	Best Practices Hidden/ "Silo'd"	Poor Morale & High Turnover	Technology & Process Gaps

There are fifteen potential problems staring back at us. Is there a way to reframe these barriers to branch success so that we can see some kind of pattern?

Here's one way: Let's organize them into groups. Which vices are most easily impacted by corporate? By the field? Which elements seem to fit together - and in what way? Do any elements tend to feed off each other?

What if we roughly organized the issues by (1) who could most effectively impact them and (2) whether they looked more like cause or effect?

A good place to start would be to identify the most intractably fixed issues, which are also the ones over which corporate has the most control. To me those look like real estate, technology and employee morale[4]. Let's start with real estate – by saying it's intractable, we mean that it's not that easy to go out and swap out 500 or 5000 locations tomorrow morning. And it's certainly not something that 500 or 5000 individual locations are going to take care of themselves tomorrow. So these are highly structural concerns over which corporate owns most or all of the control.

Why does employee morale belong here? Because morale, like real estate and technology, tends to show up in real big pictures. Sure, morale differs from place to place within a company – but the environment created and maintained by corporate is the # 1 driving force behind morale on a company-wide basis. After all, the fact that you have a bad apple managing you in St. Louis generally does not affect me in the Philadelphia office as much as if we both had a bad apple dropping on us from corporate.

Employee Morale and High Turnover recurred with such regularity in our interviews that we broke that general category into subcategories. When asked why people leave, it usually boiled down to one of three subsets: failure to invest in new skills, distance from the decision-making process, and overall attitude. These are labeled here as employee skill set, employee agility, and employee attitude.

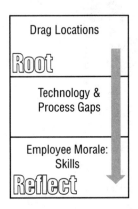

What other issues are mostly owned by the company, as opposed to being owned by individual branches? Certainly the decision-making process is an organizational feature: that is, which activities and decisions are centralized? If the <u>wrong things are centralized</u>, that leads to a culture where <u>competitors react faster to new opportunities</u>.

As employees see their company and themselves being consistently outpaced by competitors, the resulting outcome is a decline in <u>morale</u> –

and it is tied to the employees' feeling that they and their company lack the <u>agility</u> to anticipate and solve customer problems.

What about the culture gap we talked about earlier? That's a shared experience (corporate and the field share responsibility) so now we're getting toward the middle of the corporate - field spectrum.

A <u>culture gap between the corporate and field offices</u> reflects, and leads to, distrust on the part of each party. And with distrust comes unreliability in branch forecasting. And with unreliability in branch forecasting comes distrust - so it's a vicious cycle. The end of the cycle: lower employee morale as reflected in <u>attitudinal</u> challenges.

What's next? How about the <u>Lamprey Lifestyle</u>? When a branch is there just to parasitically live off its prehistoric skills (nothing new, remember), it is a prime candidate for <u>Tribal Negotiation</u>. After all, let's forget about the company, it's all about what's best for their branch, right?

This isn't totally a branch issue, though, since there may be some lampreys lurking at corporate - so let's put those boxes somewhere in the middle.

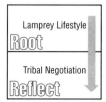

Next, we could say that a <u>stale product</u> leads to a loss of enthusiasm and thus <u>unfocused sales activity</u>. Further we might observe that unfocused sales activity leads to a general attitude of malaise and <u>noncompliance with brand standards</u>. But is a stale product really the responsibility of the branches or the corporate support center? Both, so it lands in the middle – but in a model branch organization most of your best product/service innovations are going to come from the field – or with heavy input from the field, so we'll let this lean toward the field:

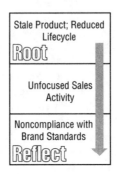

Finally, let's connect the challenges that the field absolutely has the most control over in a model organization: <u>taking the initiative to cross-sell,</u> <u>reducing opacity</u> by asking for help from those who are interested in your success, and <u>seeking and sharing those "hidden" best practices.</u>

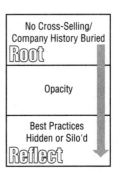

This exercise shows us one way to group these barriers to success. Shown together, they form the...

Periodic Table of Branch Vices

Periodic Table of Branch Vices

Root

Drag Locations	Wrong Things Centralized	Culture Gap between Field & Corporate		Stale Product Reduced Lifecycle	No Cross-Selling/ Company History Buried
Technology & Process Gaps	Competitors React Faster to New Opportunities	Surprises In Branch Forecasting	Lamprey Lifestyle	Unfocused Sales Activity	Opacity
Employee Morale: Skills	Employee Morale: Agility	Employee Morale: Attitude	Tribal Negotiation	Noncompliance with Brand Standards	Best Practices Hidden/ "Silo'd"

Reflect

Corporate-Centric ←————————→ Field-Centric

Is There a Model Branch?

We've considered the interesting characters we meet during our branch journey – and some of the vices that torpedo real-life branch profitability.

But what about the idea of an individual model branch? A perfect place where customers are happy, retention is strong, best practices are shared and investors are always mildly and pleasantly surprised? The land of milk and honey...

Anyone who is ever told, "This is the Model Office – you are perfect!" feels great and then starts to wonder, "What does that mean? My God, how long can I make this last?" Is there really a perpetual state of nirvana where we are loved and respected, forever protected from the arrows of competitors and the vagaries of our respective industries?

No.

Nirvana comes from a Sanskrit word meaning the "wind that blows out." It is defined as the final beatitude that transcends suffering and extinguishes the search; a goal that is hoped for but apparently unattainable[5]. If nirvana is the act of extinguishing something, I'm not sure we want to achieve that in the branch setting – that would mean we're done!

<u>There may or may not be a model branch, but there certainly is a discipline of branch modeling</u>. And that means, regardless of the condition of our branch(es) today, we can cultivate skills and results that fuel our quest to model further.

In that way, the branch is not the model – we are the model. Which taken to its logical conclusion means that the biggest branch (today) is not always the best:

- The absolute worst branch in your network can be redefined and improved if the local staff commits to branch modeling. Note: if the local market will not economically support progress regardless of effort (that's like trying to breathe underwater without scuba or snorkel), the modeling may include an analysis of whether to continue to commit resources there.

- The most profitable branch in your network may or may not be a model operation: how much of its performance is explained by short-term economic factors? And how much by local efforts to understand, improve and share best practices? Does it merely provide local cash flow? Or does it generate cash flow coupled with examples and ideas you can leverage across the organization. Is its success replicable? Or is it a mere anomaly?

We will refer to a <u>model branch</u> within the following pages – what this term refers to is the picture each person we interviewed had of a model operation in their business.

There is a great debate within many branch organizations – and it sounds like the "chicken vs. the egg" debate framed in a branch context: does one create a model branch first, then replicate its attributes over multiple locations while preserving those which have achieved nirvana? Or does one think in the context of a model organization first – how do we want our branches working together? – and then use that thinking, that collective energy and focus to continuously improve each local operation?

Leonardo da Vinci painted the *Mona Lisa*. It is a perfect, or model, painting. How would we feel if da Vinci had gone on to paint 50 more *Mona Lisa* instead of creating the *Codex Leicester*, the *Madonna of the Rocks*, or the fresco of the *Last Supper*? What if Monet, Rembrandt and

Picasso each painted 500 copies of *Mona Lisa* – after all, it is the perfect painting!

Is the *Mona Lisa* the model? Or is Leonardo da Vinci?

"Is there one model branch?" For many companies: no – not in a permanent sense. No one branch can save a company and it is rare and unhealthy for one branch to always be on top. However, the word "model" still has an important meaning in branch operations. We can model better branches – through our virtuous behavior. In this way, we become the model.

Only you can answer the question "Does a model branch really exist for your company?" We should be wary of those who blindly insist "yes" for every organization. Is it the model for today? For the next 12 months? Forever? At what point do we grow to revile what we once viewed as perfection? Maybe it is when we operate merely as "cloners."

Business is not particularly complicated – but the human mind is. So let's start with a simple idea, open our eyes to a new way of managing branch operations, and picture our model branch not as a branch, but as a method of driving us toward branch excellence. As we draw closer to that picture of our model branch, it may evolve further, becoming more attractive, and stepping ahead of us...pulling us forever towards it. Virtuous branch modeling is that process and our movement within it.

Chapter Five:

What are the 6 Virtues of a Top Performing Field Operation?

"It makes money."

"It's our oldest branch."

"It's the branch which consistently grows the fastest."

Yes, maybe, and probably. But why?

Anyone can stare admiringly at a top performer and announce the obvious. But what's behind the curtain? What fuels excellence in field operations? Why are some locations so much more productive than their peers?

Everyone has some idea of what a model branch looks like. That idea is often formed with the perspective or memory of what the top-performing operations in their own organization look like. What I was interested in throughout the interviews was whether there were any attributes common to all great branches – regardless of company or industry.

The value in identifying these common attributes – or virtues, really, since they are common sources of strength – would be to give a broader perspective to the company that is seeking to replicate its own best practices. To give ideas to the company or manager that wants to understand their own operation, but also wants to look beyond their company and beyond their industry…to test the limits of what is possible next.

Before fully understanding the virtues of top-performing offices, we need to first ask and answer the question, "**Why do we operate via the branch model?**"

When asked, "Why do you operate via the branch model?", branch personnel and executives from those organizations responded with these types of answers...

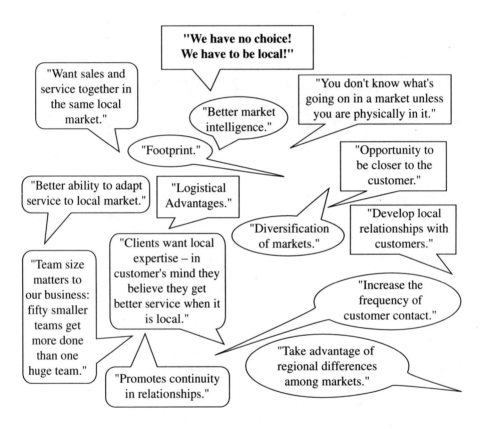

Very few respondents said, "We operate via the branch model because we know we can make 'x' % return on sales per branch, or 'y' dollars from each and every one of these offices. Our market and infrastructure will support 'z' number of branches...that's why we look like we do."

Are we telling the truth when we give "relationship reasons" for opening or maintaining branches? Sure. And if so, it looks like we open branches to serve people and to gain knowledge. But isn't it odd that we close branches for a different reason? That reason-for-close having everything to do with current profitability and very little to do with relationships, diversification, or "having to be in that market." The dollars often make the decision for us on the back end: when we close branches for financial reasons. Not saying it's right or wrong – but the reasons above all seem to go out the window when an office is slated to close.

The serious "strategic discussion" which takes place around branch-closing often involves a lot of knitted brows, pensive looks and chin-rubbing. A brief amount of discussion about people and customers. And ultimately the calculators come out – we close offices when we are losing money. Period.

Beyond the question of why companies operate via the branch model, "What virtues are shared by the very best branches?"

While there was great variety earlier in the reasons why offices fail, there was pretty close to unanimous agreement about what the winners look like:

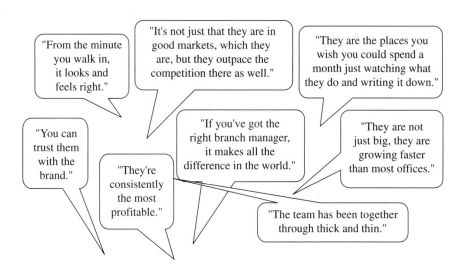

"From the minute you walk in, it looks and feels right."

"It's not just that they are in good markets, which they are, but they outpace the competition there as well."

"They are the places you wish you could spend a month just watching what they do and writing it down."

"You can trust them with the brand."

"They're consistently the most profitable."

"If you've got the right branch manager, it makes all the difference in the world."

"They are not just big, they are growing faster than most offices."

"The team has been together through thick and thin."

It is interesting that there are fewer general observations about the high-performing branches than there were about the problems we considered earlier. Greatness is sometimes simpler than mediocrity, isn't it? <u>Not easier</u>, but simpler.

The statements above come from branches in significantly different industries. But do any of them look out of place when considered in the context of your operations?

There may be some important element(s) missing here. Something unique to your business. For example, your top branches may be ISO 9002 registered. Or Sarbanes-Oxley compliant. Those requirements are unique to your business. In contrast, **the 6 Virtues shown below are universal to all great field operations**:

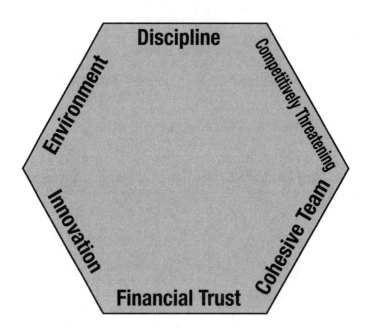

Let's take a quick look at each of these 6 Virtues and what they mean to the people working in field operations:

Environment

- Employee Selection – hiring process & criteria.
- Employee Development – focused performance management.
- Right Location – not necessarily the most expensive – or the cheapest – but demographically situated to address the most common reason for wanting a branch: "opportunity to be closer to the customer."
- Right Design – clean (no Slumlord Monkeys!), if that's important to your business. Has a flow that makes it easier for the employee to perform tasks important to the customer.
- Right Tools – systems that make it easier to do good things for the customer, and for each other.

Cohesive Local Team

- Real Leadership – not only intimately knows the functions performed within the office, but <u>sees things that others don't see today</u>. Not just a "trench buddy" that will roll up the sleeves: that alone is not leadership. Drives the local market by tapping into the company's vision.
- Problems not Delegated – employees bring problems to the manager and the manager handles them personally. Especially customer-related problems.
- Good at Decision-Making – can intelligently respond to the query, "Tell me about the most important decision you made for the branch this week."
- Low Turnover – employees stay. Not a lot of noise about "good turnover." Good in what way? That we spent time hiring, training and managing a person and all that investment is gone? Top branches hire right in the first place because the hiring process (part of Environment, Virtue # 1 above) is important to them.

Discipline

- Compliance with Brand Standards – the branch knows what they are. Knows why they are important. Understands the internal power of the brand. Views brand loyalty almost as an ethical commitment.
- Compliance with Regulatory Requirements – follows the rules related to hiring, employee relations and other areas that are legally significant to the business.
- Public and Private Compliance: as one of the executives we interviewed commented, "They don't give you public compliance and private defiance."
- Effective at New Product Rollouts because the Existing Platform is Strong – there are only as many moving parts as necessary. Which makes the introduction of a new moving part something the branch can handle.

Competitively Threatening

- Vigorously Defends Current Customer Relationships – uses a proven process to penetrate and retain key accounts.
- Not satisfied with "glowing reviews" and customer comfort, but Actively Expands Market Share – not just a great defender, an 800-lb man sitting on his sandwich ("No one can take this from me!"), but offensively acts within the marketplace as well. Which keeps competitors off-balance and out of the key accounts.
- Knows 5x to 10x More About the Competition & Accounts than Peers – uses intelligence resources, understands what is happening within key accounts and industries.

• Shorter Sales Cycle, Higher Close Ratio than Peers – sophisticated targeting and cross-selling; greater involvement of the service team in the sales process. Better than peers at getting referrals.

Financially Trustworthy

• Consistently meets or beats Financial Expectations.
• Good at Forecasting.
• Keeps Feeding the Sales Funnel.
• Understands the Financial Levers in the Business – not a one-dimensional approach to branch financial management (for example, sales only or "cut costs" only). Able to move margin and SG&A[6] when strategically important to do so.

Innovative

• Comes up with Better Ways to Do Things – one Model Office came up with a simple adjustment to the company's invoice format which contributed to a two-day reduction in the <u>company's</u> Days Sales Outstanding.
• Contributes to New Product or Service Development.
• Good at Prioritizing, so their "New Ideas" aren't just new, they Actually Impact Things that Matter.
• Able to Balance Innovation with Compliance – one without the other is no advantage. This balance is addressed in detail in the next chapter.

For a company seeking consistent advantage through its field operations, these are the six areas to document, train, monitor and reward. But where is the starting line? Which of the virtues are most important? Which of them, if any, lead to the others?

In the next chapter, we will examine the close relationship between cause and effect within these virtues. Our discoveries there will lead us to the starting line for future improvement.

Chapter Six:

What You See vs. What's Really There: 3 Reflective Virtues vs. 3 Projective Virtues

By analyzing the 15 common branch problems in Chapter Three, we were able to organize those 15 problems into a Periodic Table of Branch Vices with just six families of elements. Part of that process was separating cause from effect. That exercise has even more meaning here: we will see from a careful examination of the six virtues introduced in the last chapter that <u>all six virtues can be attained by focusing on just three of them</u> – but they have to be the right three. Here's what we mean.

Let's start by considering the road taken by most companies, most of the time – those companies focus most or all of their resources on three obvious virtues: Financial Reliability, Cohesive Local Teams with high morale, and a Threatening Competitive visage. These are tremendous virtues for any branch to possess. They are actually what we want as results. In fact, they may be all we care about – and there would be nothing wrong with that.

So it is common for companies to make the following investments...

If a company wants Financial Trust, it may invest in:	If a company wants Cohesive Local Teams, it may invest in:	If a company wants to be Competitively Threatening, it may invest in:
Frequent conference calls dedicated to forecasting[7].	Time and effort to create "good turnover."	Lead generation.
Hiring top producers away from competitors (and paying for them).	Headhunter fees.	Building a "red-meat" sales culture by tilting compensation plans heavily towards new revenue generation.
Constant analysis, ranking and color-coding of individual and branch efforts.	Resources for "newbies" at a rate disproportionate to their representation and to their contribution.	Take-away programs (dedicating disproportionate incentives to new account development).
Long-term customer contracts based on price.	Severance, litigation expense, and management training centered on risk-reduction.	Reward programs that send "top producers" to exotic locations, some of whom (the top producers) go to work for a competitor within 90 days of taking the trip!

None of these investments are inherently wrong all of the time. But their return on investment is inherently limited because they may be chasing events that have already happened. They may be swinging at shadows. It's like Leisure Suit Lenny thinking that a spray of breath mint is going to make him irresistible to the ladies. It won't hurt, but there's probably a better approach...like ditch the leisure suit and lounge lizard personality!

The three goals listed above (financial reliability, team cohesiveness & competitive vigor) are not only worthy goals, but they are reflected in the performance of the top branches with which we came into contact. So they are real virtues of top-performing branches. <u>But It Turns Out You Can Achieve These Three Virtues By Focusing Resources on the Other Three.</u>

We call Financial Reliability, Cohesive Local Team and Competitively Threatening the "Three Reflective Virtues." The "Reflective Virtues" are a reflection of a branch's relative strength. They show us today what is happening on the inside of the branch - and again, they are things we really do care about.

In contrast, the other three virtues (Discipline, Environment and Innovation) are called the "Three Projective Virtues." They do not represent a reflection of the branch - instead, they <u>project the image</u> of the branch; they are not the branch's results today, they are what the branch's core really looks like.

Many companies confuse the reflection with the branch itself: this is easy to do. When a man looks in a mirror, he thinks he sees himself. <u>But he does not see himself</u>. Instead, he sees his reflection at that moment. The difference between many companies and this man facing the mirror - the man usually doesn't get mad at the mirror if he doesn't like what he sees!

Ultimately, what we want to do is <u>improve the reflection</u> (what we see) <u>- and the branch itself</u>. We do that by wisely considering the difference between these six virtues and applying our resources to the branch's core, not just its reflection:

One way to differentiate your company is to adopt a branch modeling strategy that <u>focuses on the Projective Virtues</u> of Discipline, Environment and Innovation.

---

[8] **pro·jec·tive** (prə-jĕk′tĭv)
adj.

1. Extending outward; projecting.

2. Relating to or made by projection.

3. *Mathematics*. Designating a property of a geometric figure that does not vary when the figure undergoes projection.

www.dictionary.com

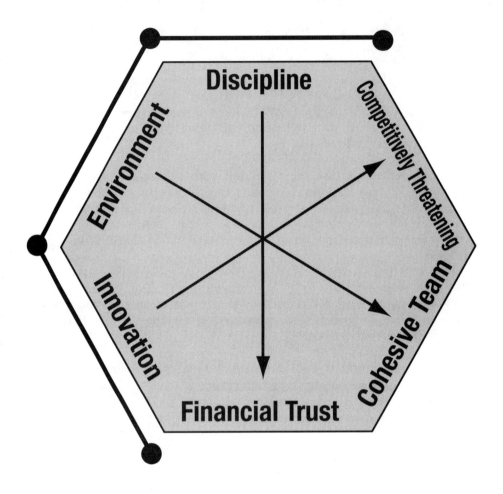

If the Reflective Virtues are "what we want," then the Projective Virtues are "what we model."

Let's examine this method. We considered a couple pages earlier how many companies "get mad at the mirror" or alternatively, "put lipstick on the mirror" in an attempt to fix their reflection instead of themselves. Here is an illustration of an alternate path. Say you want to have Cohesive Local Teams. Instead of matching the approach taken by some of your peers, invest in Environment instead. Here's how it works:

If a company wants to improve its Environment, it may invest in:	This results in the following Environmental improvement:	AND a corresponding improvement in building Cohesive Local Teams:
Retooling the hiring criteria and process to address the Projective Virtues.	Fewer bad hires; increased number of hiring "wins."	Quality people like working with quality people.
Professional site selection.	Improved customer access.	Stronger relationships between employees and customers.
Site simulation, modeling and design.	Improved workflow. Reduced "scrap" in the service process.	Less re-work and frustration.
Objective assessment of branch methods and results; certification of inside "expert class" in the branches.	Benchmarks internal quality against independent standards.	Takes the politics out of performance review.

Note: Environment is not just about hiring. I remember hearing about one company that had a model hiring process. It was strategically sound. The employees were proud of it. But there was little beyond it. So the company was able to hire a lot of A Players…and turn them into B Players. An expensive strategy, no?

Fixing team problems through modest Environmental adaptation improves both those virtues cost-effectively. It's better than putting lipstick on the mirror! Why does it matter? Because the Environment – the place we work within and the processes we use is our "home field advantage." Why do most teams, regardless of skill or competitor, tend to play better at home? What can we learn from that?

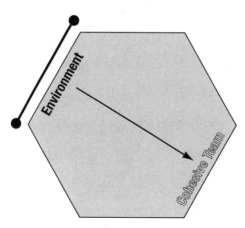

Next, let's consider the reason we're all in business: to make money. Now, there is nothing wrong with spending money on the Financial Trust tools mentioned earlier. But you can get both Financial Trust and Discipline by focusing on...Discipline.

If a company wants to improve its Discipline, it may invest in:	This results in the following Discipline improvement:	AND a corresponding improvement in building Financial Trust:
Communication and reinforcement of meaningful brand standards.	People can articulate what is most important, and see priorities more easily.	Activities that create value (and make you money) are performed with greater regularity. It doesn't get much simpler than that.
Training on how to execute brand standards.	Fewer on-the-job training errors.	Lower incidence of customer complaints; improved client retention.
Reward Programs that recognize compliance with brand standards.	Measurable progress in meeting measurable brand standards.	Should be structured in a way that (1) redirects resources proportionally toward brand-performers, and (2) keeps resources in the company (as opposed to the traditional "junket").
Independent assessments of customer satisfaction.	Takes (some of) the politics out of account review. Assess which brand standards are meaningless to the customer – and throw them out!	Service and value improve. Message more targeted. Sales cycle shortened; closing ratio improved.

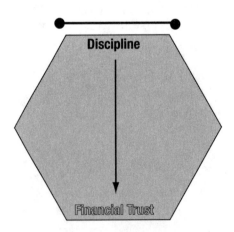

One of the reasons Discipline leading to Financial Trust is so important is that when a person works in a branch office, that person doesn't get to see the vast array of company resources that a person working on a large, corporate campus sees. If your business is one where sales calls take place at customer sites, it may be rare for your salesperson to visit a customer location as small as your branch.

So how do you create a sense of strength for your little ol' office in Aurora calling on the big prospects? Brand Strength through Discipline. That brand on the door is what your people have to hold onto when things get tough. It's what they want to feel patriotic towards. It's what they want you to Trust them with Financially.

It doesn't come just from advertising. It doesn't come just from product mix. It comes from the daily execution of those standards that say "we are serious – these things matter in every one of our "x" number of locations."

Without compliance to brand standards, you don't have a brand, you've got a watermark – and it's fading. With compliance, you have the platform for brand Discipline, which we will soon discuss further in subsequent chapters.

OK, depending on how you're counting, we're 2 for 2 (or 4 for 2!) in addressing the Virtues. What about the desire to increase market share? To beat the competition head-to-head, and to outflank them generally through branch modeling...

If a company wants to improve its Innovation, it may invest in:	This results in the following Innovation improvement:	AND a corresponding improvement in Competitive Stature:
Innovation workshops.	Best practices come out of the silos.	More weapons in more markets.
Competitive analysis partnerships.	Understanding and articulation of the true differentiators.	Makes it easier for the customer to choose you over their alternatives.
Intellectual property protection.	Patented business processes.	Proprietary advantage. Captures the ground held by "thought-leaders" in the industry.
Selective acquisitions and targeted research.	New products and services.	Addresses the burden of lifecycles that are long in the tooth.

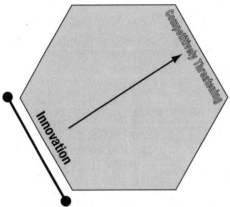

Innovators are likely to have longer branch life-cycles, better margins, and lower employee turnover. When a company gets really good at this, it reaches a level we call Composition, which we will discuss in a later chapter.

In sum, by addressing the Projective Virtues, we attain them <u>plus</u> we receive additional return on investment by attaining the Reflective Virtues as well. When done correctly (by matching proven resources to the Projective Virtues), companies see past their reflection to (1) reveal the real strengths of their branches, (2) increase the number of high-yield locations and (3) reduce the costs associated with subsidizing non-performers.

There's one last area I'd like you to consider: **the strange link between Discipline and Innovation.** Why is it strange? Well, it is counterintuitive and thus unexpected by most managers.

If you asked 100 people whether they would rather be considered to be innovative or compliant, somewhere north of 90% would say "innovative." But Innovation without a platform of Discipline provides only temporary and quickly fading benefits.

Here are three illustrations showing...

How Good Ideas Get Stuck in Average Organizations

Discipline is the "choke-point" that limits a company's ability to leverage good ideas through its branch network. Here's a diagram of a *visible choke point.*

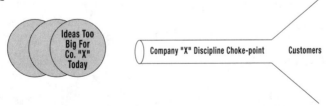

If your idea is as big as a basketball, and your Discipline platform has the circumference of a peashooter, you'll never get that good idea executed consistently through your network. <u>Not one big idea will fit</u>.

Put another way, if your Discipline platform has the circumference of a peashooter, you can only introduce new ideas that are "as big" as a pea. <u>Anything bigger has to be abandoned</u> to make room for the tiny ideas that do fit!

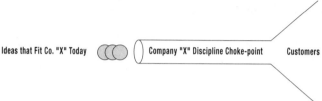

Ideas that Fit Co. "X" Today   Company "X" Discipline Choke-point   Customers

Think about the future you want for your organization. Is it limited to the next smart idea that can squeeze through your Discipline choke-point? Or do want to build a branch platform with a reputation for execution so solid that your business is bigger than any single idea that could come to it? So solid that your business can effectively promote its big idea, or lots of small ones simultaneously? If your competition is using peashooters, you may want to work on building a cannon!

Next, let's consider an *invisible choke point*. At least in the prior set of illustrations, Company X could see the circumference of its Discipline choke-point. What about the less obvious situation?

Below we can see that Company X has over-committed at the threshold, because its throughput is limited, like plaque in arteries, by the "crud" already in the pipe – the branches don't have the time or energy for a new initiative, even a small one! The smallest ideas look like they will fit, but even they will get stuck.

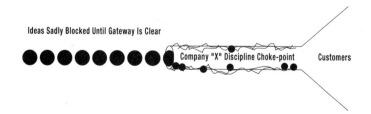

Ideas Sadly Blocked Until Gateway Is Clear

Company "X" Discipline Choke-point   Customers

Bottom line: focusing on Discipline opens your choke-point. Linking the Projective Virtues of Discipline and Innovation will let you promote bigger ideas to your customers ahead of their expectations, and ahead of the competition.

How to Beat Company "X" (shown above):

Your New Ideas | Your Discipline Choke-point | Customers

Is <u>brand discipline</u> viewed as a burden or an opportunity in your organization today?

In the next chapter, we will consider the way top-performing field locations use the Projective Virtue of Discipline as a market differentiator. This practice captures the paradox present in the best field operations: <u>synchronous differentiation,</u> which is when one is able to create a unique position in the marketplace through the consistent application of the most important brand standards: using internal <u>same-ness</u> to create a difference for their customers and employees.

Chapter Seven:
The 1st Projective Virtue is Discipline

As a consumer, think about the worst service experience you've had recently. Now think about the service standards of the organization involved: <u>can you name a single service standard of that organization</u>? Probably not.

Discipline projects financial reliability and strength, because Discipline is what drives sales and reduces waste. If a field operation is losing money, chances are it is either part of an organization with inarticulate service standards, <u>or</u> more likely, the standards are there but that location has lost its way.

What's the highlight of most operations reviews? The financials! Because the financials are important and measurable. But what about the reasons behind the financials? If we want to fix the financials, we don't talk exclusively about the financials, we talk about the activity behind them. If we want to run the mile faster, we don't talk endlessly about our last time trial: we talk about how to improve our workout session. And then we execute the improvements!

When a branch's leadership cares about Financial Trust, it focuses on the Discipline in the branch. Why? Because Discipline is the single most important aspect of branch leadership. Because Discipline proves the fit of the company's value proposition to the market's need. Because Discipline leads to Financial Trust. Because Discipline means someone local cares about the values and goals of the brand.

Think about the branches and stores you admire, within the companies whose brands really last and stand for something. We may envy their financial success, but more importantly, we admire their Discipline.

That's why, even when those companies experience the rare cyclical downturn, we see them as a "buying opportunity" rather than a "sinking ship."

It is even easier to consider in reverse…

- How long can a company with sloppy sales practices expect continued top-line growth, or even maintenance?
- How quickly will cavalier operating practices increase costs and destroy margins?
- Does market share find companies with a reputation for consistent execution or fire-fighting?
- Without a common language and practices, what chance does communication have?

Take apart the word Discipline and you find the word, "disciple." That's not an accident. Inside the word, "disciple" is the root "sci" from scienter, meaning deliberately or knowingly. In other words, by definition, you can't be an accidental disciple.

What does one have to know to be a disciple? It varies from business to business. And that knowledge variance is what defines the differentiation between those businesses. Differences in patient treatment options and procedures define the quality of the experience at a nursing home. Manufacturing processes define the quality of a product. Understanding the customers' needs at the design stage helps define future market acceptance.

Why does Discipline matter?

Because it drives Financial Trust. It's fruitless to complain about the financial results to people who don't understand what actions generate revenue and who don't perform them with consistency. That's just an emotional exercise – it doesn't solve anything.

How are the current compliance levels in your field operations affecting Growth in Same Store Sales? If sales activity is subpar, you are no doubt behind budget. If service standards are optional, you are leaving the top line to chance.

How does Discipline improve quality & reduce waste? If the right money-making activities, or "magic moments[8]" aren't performed with reliable accuracy, you're probably experiencing more than your fair share of refunds and disputed bills.

How does Discipline enhance the brand? A brand today is associated with marketing, but its original meaning was one of ownership. That original meaning is not lost on your customers. They don't want to know your brand for marketing purposes. They want to know who owns what the brand is attached to. So they can affix blame when something goes wrong!

Inside a field location, Discipline is what defines whether you really have a brand - or just a "melting pot" of casual, uncoordinated effort. In the subsequent section observing Discipline, we will consider actual pitfalls and differentiators in the areas that matter:

Brand Standards & The Role of Training

Recognizing & Rewarding Brand Discipline

Testing Marketplace Acceptance via Global Commitments

Community Standards (Legal/Regulatory Compliance)

In the end, you know what matters to your customers. But how do you know? And how do your people know? How are the things that matter reinforced in your company today? Is there an opportunity for greater clarity? How do you know if there is a Discipline opportunity? Take a look at the Periodic Table of Branch Vices: if your organization is experiencing issues in the <u>center squares</u>...there is a Discipline opportunity.

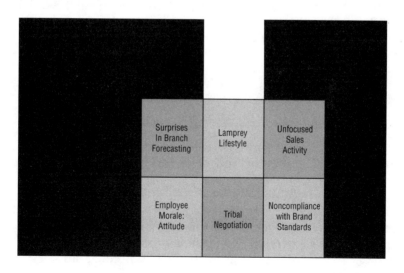

| Surprises In Branch Forecasting | Lamprey Lifestyle | Unfocused Sales Activity |
| Employee Morale: Attitude | Tribal Negotiation | Noncompliance with Brand Standards |

Why does addressing these center squares matter? Because they drive financial reliability: a field operation cannot become financially reliable if it is sloppy.

Discipline Fuels Financial Trust

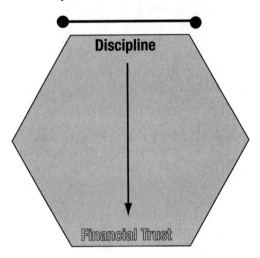

How would you rate the attendance and punctuality in your field operations? The compliance with brand standards? Sales activity? If attendance and the brand standards are just casually important, your salespeople probably aren't very excited about promoting the company. And with the resulting gap in sales activity comes…eroding top line and weaker gross margins.

Is each month a surprise when it comes to forecasting? Are your average branches having a hard time seeing the greater good? Are they more interested in turf protection (tribal negotiation) than in collective progress or healthy competition? Are they living off the same customer demographic?

One of the key differentiators between great branches and also-rans is that their level of Discipline and compliance with brand standards is obvious to even the casual observer.

What does the Projective Virtue of Discipline look like? It's not handcuffs and rules – to the contrary, it looks like energy: strong morale, positive feelings, pride of ownership. To the customer, it looks like consistency and caring. To the sales manager, it looks like predictable sales activity and predictable results.

Interviews with branch professionals indicate that this is really the cornerstone virtue; it is the hardest virtue to obtain – and the one that leads to the most enduring results. Where there is a lack of Discipline, who cares where your operation is located or how many new ideas they come up with?

The best location and site design in the world cannot save a sloppy branch. And the best ideas won't come from sloppy branches, because sloppy branches take shortcuts that feel good to themselves, instead of to the customers.

Based on the feedback from people in field operations, the evidence of Discipline speaks to whether the branch is highly effective, or merely shuffling along. The best offices differed from the middle-of-the-road offices in the following Discipline factors:

✔ Customers Understand the Company's Brand Standards for Service
✔ The Site Understands the Concept of Service Redline (more information on this subject can be found in the subsequent chapter on New Product Impact Testing)
 - When and how long are the peak periods?
 - What are we doing during the slow periods?
✔ Sales Standards Clearly Articulated to & Executed by Sales Force
 - Show me your Job Description; what do you think we expect of you?
 - Show me your Calendar.
 - Explain any deviation (does the company's sales activity standard need to be adapted?)
 - Who is our Target Prospect?
 - Why would they want to do business with us?
 - Why hasn't this one started yet?
✔ Service Standards Clearly Articulated & Executed to Service Team
 - Show me your Job Description.
 - Show me what you are working on today.
 - How would a Customer have filled out your last Performance Evaluation?
 - Describe the process you use to fill a customer request.
✔ Technology Applied to Customer Development & Problem-Solving
 - Show me how you are recording customer activity.
 - What do you think I ought to be able to learn about this operation from a brief visit here?
 - Is any of that information recorded where I can access it remotely?

This is followed by a close examination of the company-specific brand standards. One litmus test for establishing whether current brand standards are adequately communicated is to compare the amount of time evaluating performance (diagnosis) vs. the amount of time improving performance (healing). It should be quickly apparent where there are activity-shortfalls. That diagnosis should take 10% of the time. The other 90% should then be spent on "healing" under-performers.

If half the time is spent on diagnosis, you've done something far worse than cut into treatment time. You've complicated the employee's job so much that they won't ever instinctively know whether what they are doing is helping the company.

Discipline is hard work, not because it forces people to do things they don't want to do, but because it requires clarity and value in the modeling – the things you say are important must really be important or you'll lose people.

Discipline isn't just about <u>doing</u> – it's starts with knowing what to do! How can a company discern whether its people know what is important today?   Compare these current messages with what would really differentiate the company. Maybe there's a great fit, maybe not...

- Executive correspondence to the field: what does it say and when was it?
- What's the first topic on regularly scheduled conference calls?
- Where is the greatest spend in training?
- Does the company website whisper, "We exist." Or is there something more?
- Is more time spent discussing customer problems or internal problems?
- What group of employees has the highest turnover? Are they properly valued?
- Which of your brand standards does your competition find most threatening?

Innovation and its reflection, Competitively Threatening, are discussed in the chapter after next. Before we get there, we need to examine the Environment: it's where our ideas meet our execution, where Discipline and Innovation make fast friends or die of disinterest.

Chapter Eight:

The 2nd Projective Virtue is Environment

When I interviewed Emilio Umeoka of Microsoft Brazil, he suggested that the way field operations can be used is changing dramatically. Where "the branch" used to be a place for the locals to use as home base, the branch now needs to be part of the customer experience, not just the employee's experience. Where "the store" used to rely on inventory, merchandising and marketing, with a little tactical sales training rolled in, the store now needs to consider how to sell to customers that won't ever walk in the door.

The Projective Virtue of Environment is all about using your space as your strength, not just as the place you accidentally happen to keep inventory or base your sales from. Top-performing field locations almost can't be separated from the Projective Virtue of their Environment, because the Environment is what is driving customer traffic (a new concept to many traditional field sales offices); it's the processes which define the customer experience (from hiring to service execution) and tools used to streamline the customer's experience.

While it's true that even a company with just one location has an Environment, this book is addressed to the businesses trying to create the Projective Virtue of Environment across multiple locations. This is a challenge because many customers have a bias against the multi-site operator: "That's a chain!" This isn't limited to restaurant discussions, by the way. Attorneys in high profile firms often resent the "branch" label assigned to their office because they don't want to feel like they're part of an outpost of an organization, where the real decision-making takes place elsewhere.

I've talked to a lot of people who hate the experience of dining or shopping at "a chain." People don't want to live in a town full of chains. Men and women bemoan the loss of local mom-and-pop businesses to the big chains. But there's not a whole lotta mom-and pops putting the big guys out of business: it's usually the other way around. Why do customers <u>hate</u> the chain in concept but patronize it in reality?

The strength of the chain is also its weakness: consistency. Consistency on its own is not a virtue. What is consistent? That your customers know what they are getting – are they bored <u>yet</u>? <u>The fact that your margins are under pressure</u>? That your employee turnover consistently runs at 100%? *That you're losing 1.1 customers for every one you bring in?*

We live in an entertainment-focused culture that values dynamism and risk-taking. "Chain" at its worst implies unoriginality. Bland, lowest common denominator service. A lack of entrepreneurial spirit. "At least I know what I'm getting…" Even the chains seem to know this: you've eaten in chain restaurants that decorate with antiques for a "one-of-a-kind look," even as they open their 1000th location. Who's kidding who?

The best field operations don't try to fake out the customer: instead, they know the advantages of scale and they're not shy about promoting them. "Lower Prices." "Better Selection." Think about scale for a minute: who is in a better position to determine location and site design for a dentist's office – the dentist who has signed three leases in his entire practice or the dental services company that operates 200 locations? It depends whether the dental services company is making use of its experience, but if it is, it is winning the experience contest.

What about the multi-site operator that ignores the advantages of scale?

The Discovery Channel attracts more viewers than the community access channel because it uses scale to its advantage. Nordstrom attracts more shoppers than the boutiques in town because of its reputation for service and selection. IBM hires better people than the local computer store because it specializes in using the brand to advance the hiring process.

Those are some of the advantages of scale.

Who should be better at hiring: the local owner who has hired 10 people, or the top branch organizations that have hired thousands? But when's the last time you heard a national operator brag, "We are better at hiring than the little guy."?

Who made the eyeglasses you are wearing? A local optometrist or a chain? Did it take three days or three hours to get them? And here I thought you were pulling for the little guy…

Why do you order a pizza from a kid with 10 minutes experience instead of ordering from the immigrant with 200 years of pizza experience in his blood? Maybe because you want the pizza in 30 minutes. Maybe because you have the choice of four local locations to choose from. Maybe because the "chain" has a better guarantee or their pizzas are hotter when they arrive.

Whatever the reason, if you are the chain competing with the local guy, you have to give the customer a reason to prefer you: because the customer's first instinct is NOT to prefer you. Their bias is for mom and pop, not you.

Why would you shop at a BIG BOX hardware store instead of patronizing Old Jerry who sold you a nut to replace the one that fell off your handlebars as a kid? Better selection. Lower prices. Closer location. Faster service (maybe!). You insensitive lout – don't you care about Jerry's family?

Why would you pay 5 - 10% more for an airline ticket on your preferred carrier instead of the low-fare alternative? Inclusion in a rewards system? Possibility of an upgrade?

Bottom line: Environment, properly applied, can level the playing field with respect to the customer's preference for working with the little guy. Bigger means you start from behind in the eyes of most consumers. And you should start from behind; Americans hate bureaucratic bloat and when an organization gets bloated enough, people seek other alternatives to doing business with it.

So where do you find your advantages in scale?

Think for a moment of your remote site locations as satellites. Which Environmental factors are most important in determining survival within those satellites?

- Location
- Site Design
- Employee Selection Process
- Employee Migration Routes from branch-to-branch
- Technology Choices

Coincidentally, these Environmental factors represent the three biggest spends in most field-driven operations: personnel expense, information technology systems, and real estate commitments.

Why does the Environment matter?

Because it drives the development of cohesive local teams, a virtue commonly found within high-performing locations.

How do your branches' Environments affect Growth in Same Store Sales? How do your branches' Environments Improve Quality and Reduce Waste? Do your branches' Environments enhance the brand?

In the subsequent section observing Environment, we will consider actual pitfalls and differentiators in the areas that matter:

Site Selection & Design
Employee Selection
Employee Migration
Technology

What are the signs of Environmental decay? To find out, you might consider talking to an expert that's seen 25,000 locations.

We just talked about the customer's perceived preference for working with the little guy over the big guy. And how that perception morphs into resignation and then brand loyalty to the big guy.

Well there's another area where the big guy has a disadvantage: only the large, distributed organization makes technology choices on a colossal enough scale to make huge mistakes. One global services company writes off almost $100 million in new systems development that went awry...and survives. One $70 billion service sector we examined has spent billions of dollars as a sector upgrading its technology...the outcome: increased perception of that industry as a commodity-provider. That's what the technology bought! Lower margins and no improvement in perception by the customer.

It boggles the mind to consider the scale of error that a large company can make...and survive in the process!

Which branch problems tend to arise or suggest Environmental decay? The ones on the left side of the Periodic Table of Branch Vices:

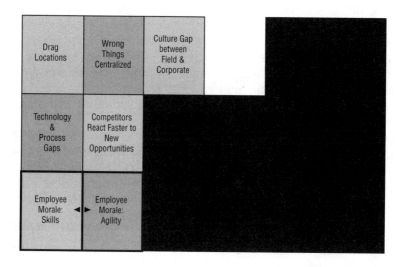

Why does addressing the left side of the Table matter? Because you build team loyalty by designing an arena with team needs, and the needs of their customers, in mind. People can get a cup of coffee anywhere. Why do so many people prefer Starbucks today?

The Environment Is Your Home-Field Advantage

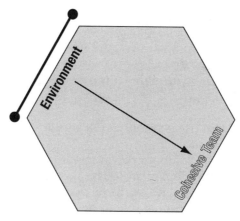

The Projective Virtue of Environment helps determine employee retention and customer awareness. The field Environment is the place where things happen.

And because local markets will always demand some level of inconsistency and freedom, your use of the Environment is a way to keep the branches from Going Native, that is, abandoning the brand standards that are important to scalability in your business.

Retail and B2B operations with customer traffic gain obvious advantages when they create an Environment that contributes positively to the customer experience. And even if you currently experience zero customer traffic, the Environment matters – it's where your people work. A sound Environmental strategy, combining employee selection with site and tools (technology) management, will reduce the costs associated with employee turnover and customer acquisition/retention.

One of the challenges in field operations is creating a Home Field Advantage in more places than one. Without the Home Field Advantage, every sales call, every customer request, every management issue becomes an Away Game. With Home Field Advantage, you create a cultural safe zone, where your people actually feel the strength of their affiliation with your company.

Having personally managed branch operations in 20 states and the District of Columbia, I've seen certain Environmental factors that were inescapably obvious during regional visits. The factors can form the basis of an Environmental Checklist; you can customize this list to address the unique needs of your organization. The best offices differed from the middle-of-the-road offices in these Environmentally significant ways:

✔ Hiring Criteria
- Show me the Hiring Criteria you are using for any open positions.
- Show me how the candidates you are interviewing "fit" the company's Hiring Criteria.
- Explain any deviation (does the company's Hiring Criteria need to be adapted?)

✔ Hiring Process
- Show me the dated notes in our applicant files.

✔ Employee Development
- What kind of feedback are you giving your people right now?
- Anything we need to document today?
- Who is scheduled to receive performance reviews this month?
- Show me a copy of the most recent performance review you conducted.

✔ Physical Workplace
- What is the first impression visitors get from the physical space?
- Does it appear safe?
- Is the office/location clean?
- Is company signage consistent with brand standards?

✔ Customer Traffic
- Tell me about your current customer traffic.

- How could we leverage increased customer traffic into greater sales?
✔ Customer Information?
  - Show me a copy of the files you keep on your most important customers.
  - Show me your Reading File (copies of any correspondence sent to customers).
  - How are company systems used to accelerate sales and improve quality?
  - How is technology used to improve the customer experience?

What do your top competitor's best field operations look like? How are they using people, real estate and technology to seduce your customers? To get them to cheat on you?

In the chapter written with Todd Ordal ("The Branch of the Future"), we start out by considering the patent awarded to a large financial services company. The patent is on their branch design. What about <u>your</u> operation today is so novel and unique that it could survive a patent application? The answer is the basis for what should be replicated in your branch Environments.

How do you get started? By recognizing that having great products or services is not enough – the consumer can often shop for those on-line. If it was only about the product, there'd be only one Ferrari dealership in North America. The local auto dealership isn't just a place to buy a car; it's also a tangible advertisement for the product. You drive by it every night and think, "What if...?"

Environmentally virtuous branches communicate to the market that you don't just have something for sale that's attractive, but that your company offers the best experience while acquiring that product or service.

The Environment is where your new ideas, your Innovation, will live or die. In the next chapter, we'll examine how the best branches create opportunities for the whole enterprise.

Chapter Nine:
The 3rd Projective Virtue is Innovation

"What's new?"

Isn't the very worst answer to that question, "n-u-t-h-i-n"?

"Nothing new" means sales are dependent solely on current customer applications and goodwill. Nothing new means margins are under pressure. Nothing new means your employees are getting bored and your customers are starting to look at you like a commodity, maybe a good commodity, but a commodity nonetheless. Sadly, few commodities retain an air of quality (gold and platinum come to mind, but only due to scarcity).

Here's what's in store for the aging product or service that is commonly available:

Stale Product + No Scarcity = Dropping Value

This problem is particularly dangerous in the distributed field network because while your message is depreciating, your personnel, real estate and technology expense commitments are staring back at you saying, "Hey you gotta pay us!" The typical reaction to this financial tug-of-war is: "Sell, sell, sell!!!" Which translates in the marketplace to "Noise, noise, noise!!!" When market acceptance is dropping across the board (meaning you and your competitors are affected equally), you can't scream at the market to drive acceptance. Why would you use that approach on your sales force under those circumstances?

The thinking sales driver will incorporate something new into the sales message. A new application, new product development, service enhancements. Something that clears the air again and gets the company out of "Me Too" status.

In the chapter on Branch Problems, I referred to the Rainbow of Life and Death when describing the problem of "Stale Product." This visual is so strong that it's worth repeating in the same place where we are talking about solving the problem.

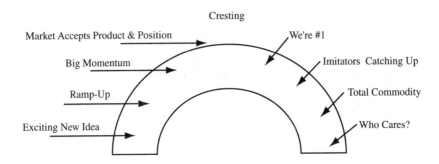

On the Rainbow of Life and Death, when should a company start thinking about the Projective Virtue of Innovation? No later than Stage Two or Three. As discussed in the upcoming chapter on New Product Impact Testing, it takes time to roll out Innovation that translates to profits and customer loyalty. Some companies are actively tuned to possibilities and wait for the new idea to strike them. Others commit to a number of new rollouts per a specific time period. Whatever the approach, an awareness of the importance of this Projective Virtue is critical.

Talk is cheap, however. Is there any organization that actively promotes a hatred of Innovation? Other than the Luddites, no! So if everyone is so committed to this wonderful concept, why are so many companies struggling with Stale Product Syndrome? It's kind of like sales, motherhood and apple pie. Everybody says they're for them, but not every company is growing its sales. And not every mother gets the attention she deserves...and when's the last time you ate a homemade apple pie?

How many patents does a business hold on its business processes? None? Hmm. How many patent applications are pending on its new ideas? How about something a little easier? Trademarks? Copyrights? If activity in these areas is flat, maybe there's an opportunity to improve that company's commitment to Innovation.

The good news is that companies, by their nature, have the Innovative gene in their DNA. Every successful company started with one new idea. When you operate field locations, you expect that your one new idea will be attractive to more than one market at the same time. But not so attractive that customers are satisfied with a purely long-distance relationship: that is why your field exists, to satisfy local hunger for your not-quite-irresistible products and services, to put inventory and decision-making closer to your customers.

More good news: your customers have Innovation in their DNA as well. Their business is changing. They are feeling pain. They are looking for a balm to soothe their pain. They want to capitalize on opportunities not currently available to them. Feeling all warm and fuzzy yet? Here's the wet blanket – they won't care about your Innovation. Not unless it solves their problem in a way that they can't just as easily remedy themselves.

Meaningful Innovation is important because it inoculates your local customers (and your employees) from boredom. It keeps customers from getting restless, from demanding lower and lower prices, from abandoning you. It keeps employees engaged, feeling like they are part of something competitive, keeps them from abandoning you.

Why does Innovation matter? Can you grow same-store sales without it? Can you improve quality or enhance the brand without any new ideas?

Innovation determines competitive strength. No one says, "Wow, thanks for repeating the same old message over and over. I was too stupid to get it the first hundred times I heard it! Now that you're here, what can I order from you!"

In the subsequent section observing Innovation, we will consider actual pitfalls and differentiators in the areas that matter:

Replicating Best Branch Practices
Branch Intelligence
New Product Impact Testing
Balancing Innovation with Compliance

How does a company know if it has an Innovation deficit? Internally, the clues are found at the right side of the Periodic Table of Branch Vices, and remember, that's the side of the table that is most closely connected to the field, not corporate.

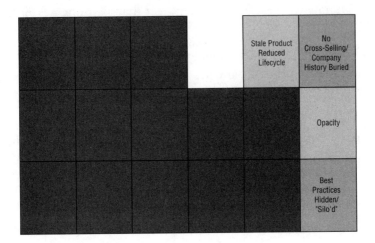

Why is it important to address the right side of the Table? Because while it is true that corporate must create a culture that fosters new development, it's ultimately the field locations that suffer most from a lack of new ideas. They feel weak and undernourished when battling for market share without any new ideas.

Creative People Win More Market Share

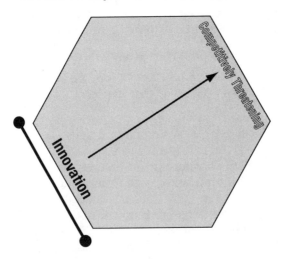

For the projective virtues of Discipline and Environment, we reviewed some sample checklists that identify differences between top-performing field operations and also-rans. But there's no checklist here for Innovation. There is a process that can be used to execute new product development, after the idea has been introduced. We discuss it in the upcoming chapter on New Product Impact Testing.

The concept development stage is uniquely structured to meet the needs of product or service, market leader or challenger, other current offerings. An Innovation Workshop should be tailored to fit the unique needs of its participants. The goal is to begin evolving from primitive Innovation, "this might work!" to sophisticated composition, which is the difference between whistling a blues riff and writing a symphony.

One of the early exercises in such a workshop is to establish the current compliance choke-points or alternative delivery channels for the organization. A company doesn't want to establish complex new practices, the girth of which exceed the company's ability to deliver. In order for a symphony "to work" it needs to be written in a language understood by the performers. In sum, Innovation cannot be separated from Discipline and Environment, nor can it exist without them.

Chapter Ten:
The First 100 Days

FT: Linda, tell us a little about your background.

LM: Frank, my first job was in a branch-based business. I worked for a high-end residential architectural firm that had offices in Orange County, Chicago, Washington, D.C., Japan, and Malaysia. I was hired to be the Marketing Director, which meant I was involved in new business development, creation of marketing collateral, and client development. I worked for that firm for eight years – and I was very fortunate to have formed a lot of my business philosophy there: it was an extremely well-run company and I learned a lot from them.

Subsequent to that relationship, I've held sales and marketing leadership roles within a variety of industries, ranging from one of the largest privately held sports complexes in North America to the mortgage industry to commercial staffing. My tenure with each company has averaged five years.

This chapter was written in cooperation with Linda McCluskey.

Ms. McCluskey is a Regional Vice President with Accounting Principals, Inc. Accounting Principals is a division of MPS Group, a billion-dollar company with offices located throughout North America, Europe and the UK.

Ms. McCluskey serves as a founding member of the Branch Productivity Institute's BPI Congress.

I am currently about 100 days into my current position as a Vice President for the Western Region of a professional staffing company.

FT: How would your peers and co-workers at those companies describe you?

LM: Sales-oriented. Driven. Results-oriented. Straightforward. Confrontational.

FT: What do you mean by confrontational?

LM: Not shy to confront issues or problems. Not afraid to suggest new or different ideas.

FT: Without revealing anything confidential, what can you tell us about the "starting point" in your different positions?

LM: Well, with the exception of the architectural firm, each position required me to take a part of a company that should have been highly profitable, but was not. For example, in the position immediately preceding this one, I led an area that was losing money – despite the fact that it should have been making money – and I made the changes necessary to turn it into the most profitable area in the company. That's what I do.

As far as a starting point, here's what I've seen when I walked into an unsuccessful area:

- It's devoid of effective local leadership, and probably has been for some time. There's no communication between offices.
- No structured communication between regions – and that's understandable because what successful region elsewhere wants to spend a lot of time talking to people who are losing money?
- There's no profile of who to hire or why. There probably was a corporate profile, but it was ignored by the local leadership and that's why they're not there anymore.
- No measurements of who to retain, or why.
- No expectations being enforced for the local people.
- And no systems in place operationally, so each branch in that unsuccessful unit is operating independently and is isolated.

FT: For a person with your background, what attracts you to these turnaround situations?

LM: Well, for me "turnaround" isn't even a strong enough word. I am clear with people that we are not just turning something around. We are taking an unsuccessful part of the business and changing it into a successful business, usually the most successful part. There are two reasons I enjoy my current role.

One, I like taking something that was a loser and making it a winner. When you do it well, as my teams have over the years, you usually get a bigger opportunity the next time around – bigger geographically, bigger revenue responsibility, bigger challenges. And that's great because then you have the opportunity to learn even more, which contributes to your professional growth and development.

Two, I really liked Jeff, the President of the company I just came to work for. I liked his philosophy. He understands the business and the importance of the people working in the branches. Not just in a lip-service kind of way, he really places a high value on the person behind the desk and their relationships.

FT: How did you accelerate your learning curve in each of these new situations?

LM: The way I accelerate the learning curve is I start early: before I have the job. Before any of these positions, I made sure I had a thorough understanding of the company, its industry, the people I would report to, the people who would report to me.

The way I got that understanding was through online research, offline research, and lots of interviews. Just prior to taking this position, I was being pursued by a very well-known national company and I stopped the interview process cold because I wanted more interviews than they were willing to give. I couldn't work at a place like that.

I also talk to professional mentors whose feedback I trust. When I was just getting into the staffing industry, I registered with ten services just to see how they treated their associates. Then I applied only with the companies that demonstrated a high level of concern for their associates.

Once I'm on the job, I've found the best way to accelerate the learning curve is to devour all the financial and client information I can get my hands on. From Day One, actually before Day One, I touched base with all the people I'd talk to during the interview process.

FT: What kinds of questions are you asking at that point?

LM: Where is the revenue coming from? What types of clients? Which products? I needed to understand the profile of who our customer was and what they were buying. In the offices, I would ask people, "What are the key factors to your success here?" Help me understand the key issues. Who are our top clients and competitors? In front of customers,

I would ask, "What factors led you to decide to do business with us?" Why are you still doing business with us? How can we make this better for both of us?

FT: Is there any advantage that the "new person" can exploit?

LM: Absolutely. You have no preconceived opinions or prejudice. No loyalties, no risk in uncovering problems – because you didn't create them!

Another advantage is that people are sometimes not as afraid as they should be. People said things to me in the first week that they would not consider saying now...because they now know me well enough to know the actions I will take.

FT: What are the key areas you looked to change in the first 100 days?

LM: There are two key areas. First you fix the WHO, then you fix the WHAT.

FT: Tell me what you mean by that.

LM: In every company I've worked, with the exception of the architectural firm, I had to turn unsuccessful offices into successful offices. And the people, the WHO, were the key to my success every time. I choose people that model a strong work ethic, character, and drive. People that can handle the rigorous demands necessary to create success. If people either could not or would not contribute to that success, I got rid of them. If they were willing and able to contribute, I didn't just stop there and give them a hug, I made sure they were in the right positions and then we worked very hard together to create success.

Next, I like to evaluate our product's intersection with our local client base, what I refer to as the WHAT. You have to be brutally honest and focused on finding an area where we can be the best. No one can be the best at everything. So I've had to make decisions that were unpopular, sometimes even at odds with a company's philosophy of "one-stop shopping." You know what happens when a company wants to compete with everyone else on a commodity basis, just so they can be one-stop? They kind of get their wish...customers shop once, then they stop shopping with you! In thousands of customer meetings, I've never once heard a customer say "I'll accept mediocrity as long as it's convenient." Maybe they're out there, I don't know. If they are, I don't want to work with them because I know I'll eventually only be competing on price.

I believe in finding a niche and driving it so hard you become known as the absolute best. It's amazing how many can't even say that, let alone try executing it. That's why you need to focus on the WHO and the WHAT during the first 100 days.

FT: What resources within your company did you use most heavily during the first 100 days?

LM: Only two, really. The president (my boss) and the human resources department.

The president because I needed his support during what proved to be a challenging time for the offices.

The human resources department because I was addressing people issues. People are the most important component and need to be addressed first. And that takes a lot of involvement on the part of HR, whether it is in facilitating new hires or terminations.

I also used the president and HR to understand what other successful people and processes were in place throughout the company, so I could replicate them in my region.

FT: What was your expectation of management over the first 100 days?

LM: Especially when you are taking over an unsuccessful area, where changing the WHO is going to be necessary, you know a lot of those people are going to be calling corporate. And when they made that call, I wanted it absolutely clear that the company was supporting me. Let's face it, change and uncertainty are difficult – having management support is critical so underperformers don't think they can just ride it out.

FT: What elements of the business did you leave alone in the first 100 days?

LM: Anything outside of my immediate realm of focus. If it wasn't the WHO or the WHAT in my region, I couldn't get as involved as I would, say later in the game. It is easy to get dragged into other operational areas – and they are often important areas: development projects, technology conference calls. Over the long term, these things contribute to the health of the company in a big way. But I could not afford to participate in them until I got to know my people and my customers. And my president backed me on that.

FT: When recruiting and hiring during the first 100 days, what did you tell new recruits about the mission at hand?

LM: I tell them that in an unsuccessful branch, you can be an Impact Player. If you have an entrepreneurial nature, if the idea of creating success gets you excited, this is the right place. If you like to ride along on something that is already working, this is not for you.

I ask for specific examples of how they impact change at the branch and customer level.

I interview the way I want to be interviewed. I want all the lumps and bruises showing during the interview. No surprises.

FT: What has surprised you during some of your first 100 days?

LM: Once you build a solid team and you get used to working with them every day, it's easy to forget the average level of commitment floating around out there in the workplace. So it's always a surprise to find poor work ethic, the degree of apathy and unprofessionalism, the lack of focus.

When there has been a lack of strong leadership on a local level, the good people have usually left. There are always exceptions to that, but they are the exceptions rather than the rule. A poor manager never leaves a fully functional team behind. Never.

FT: Anything you wished you had done differently in the past 100 days?

LM: Always trust your gut. Especially regarding work ethic, character and commitment.

FT: How will the next 100 days be different from the first 100?

LM: We'll focus more now on the WHAT. My first week, I held a conference call where we identified our four constituencies: our shareholders, our clients, our internal team and our contractors. And I asked, "What are each of you doing to positively impact these four constituencies today?" We'll do even more of that now that we've got the beginnings of a good team in place.

I think in a branch-based business, it really matters what kind of people you have out there building relationships, understanding the goals, going beyond their own motivation and thinking about how to motivate clients.

FT: At the end of this year, how will you have differentiated your business from its competitors?

LM: We will have better people. And they will be performing better than their peers elsewhere.

FT: Every company in the world claims they have the best people. How are you going to prove it to the people that matter?

LM: We've talked about this before, Frank, so you know I don't mean "better people" in some kind of "Kumbaya, we're all wonderful and better than everyone else because we say we are." I mean these people are the most profitable and the fastest growing – their results prove the assertion that they're better.

Another way is to step back and ask, "Why in the world would the best people want to work here?" And it's the reasons you write about in your research...Do our branches have the Discipline to establish and live up to brand standards? What kind of Environment have we created – how are we investing in our people? Is there anything being created or composed here? With the right answers to those questions, you won't even have to tell the marketplace you've got the best people, the marketplace will already know it.

At the time this book went to press, the First 100 Days had passed. Here were Linda's results from that short period of time:

- *80% of the branches have grown sales over the same month, same quarter, and YTD from prior year.*
- *In this turnaround region, where no individual branch was making money at the outset, 50% of the branches were posting profits after 100 Days.*
- *Operating cost as a % of sales dropped by six percentage points.*
- *3 new branches are scheduled to open in the next 100 Days.*

Chapter Eleven:

Developing Virtuosity Through Your Own Branch University

How much "higher learning" do you actually use to generate results in your business? How well did college prepare you to successfully manage field operations?

Which class taught you to say, "thank you" to a customer?
How about, "I'm sorry. Let me fix that for you."
Where did you learn the importance of saying "I appreciate you"?
Which test asked you "True or False…your career depends on the people you work with"?

I don't remember learning those things from a college textbook, do you? I can remember a few of the course titles from my undergraduate days (including Highlights of Astronomy and Politics of the Middle East!). Thinking that maybe the curriculum has changed for the better, I checked out the titles of some classes currently posted on the web as examples of college curricula:

Universalism Ungendered
Politics & Identity
Legacy of the Modern World
Culture and the Social Experience
Social Analysis

Not to mention entire degree programs available in Ancient Studies, Cinema Studies and Gender & Sexuality Studies (those three from an Ivy League institution that puts the words "useful knowledge" in quotes on its home page). That's what those lucky enough to get a liberal arts education are learning today before going to work at your company. All terrific programs, but maybe not immediately relevant to your field operations.

Let's compare those learning opportunities to the classes I wish I could have taken as a Branch Manager during my first year on the job:

- How to differentiate yourself during a sales call.
- How to reduce the risk in hiring new people.
- Which reports matter…and which don't.
- How to prioritize values and activities, especially directives coming from corporate.
- When something's not working, when to give up and when to hold your ground.
- How to tell when your company is in trouble.
- How to get better and better at employee development and performance reviews.
- How to grow gross margin faster than expenses.
- How to match people's skills and interests with your site's needs.

I'm not sure if I could have found those courses anywhere. But I know I could teach some of those courses today (the branch ones, not the ungendered ones!) – and we've all met people we could learn even more from.

And that's the point, isn't it? To give employees the opportunity to learn from each other, not from a smarmy bluenose with a bunch of initials after his or her name. <u>To give employees the opportunity to teach each other. To give employees a safe place to challenge the existing processes and question whether there really is a better way</u>.

How about including customers in the learning process? Maybe we'd stop boring customers to death if we spent less time in sales calls talking about the fish on the wall and more time sharing the things we are learning about our relationships with them.

If you don't think an employee's loyalty will be boosted when you ask him or her to teach others what they know, you've got the wrong kind of people working for you. And not only do you get more loyalty, but there was already some there to start with.

<u>I never had a college professor who cared how much money I would make</u>. But I have learned a lot from mentors who had a personal stake in my financial success – as every manager should!

What can you start to teach in your organization? How about…

Discipline
Environment
Innovation

What does Discipline 101 look like at your company? What could you and your team develop that into? What common language could you use to link brand standards together?

How about Innovation Labs? A place where the scientific method is used to propose and evaluate new and better ways to serve the customer? Don't let the word "science" scare you off. It's related to the words disciple and discipline. And science is so underutilized in business problem-solving that a minimal commitment to it will measurably reduce whining and hopelessness.

What is an office or store supposed to look like at your company? How are people supposed to be hired and developed in that Environment? That's Environment 101. If you don't have Environment 101, think about who can help you get it. If you do have it, but it doesn't seem to be making a difference, change it!

The good news in all this: you don't have to start from Square One. There are ways to integrate proven methodologies in sales, service and administration into your Discipline, Environment and Innovation curriculum.

In an upcoming chapter on training and certification, we'll consider some observations on learning methodology from two executives at the world's leading sales training company. To avoid redundancy, I won't address the insource/outsource dichotomy here, but it should be said that there is a real science to design and delivery of continuous learning modules. Consider their expert perspective when deciding what components to design internally and how to use third party experience as a way to speed delivery and improve benchmarking.

Branches are usually managed by regional geography, but their needs differ according to the various stages in their lifecycles, not according to geography.

So where do you start?

And what types of continuing education opportunities make the most sense for a start-up, for a turnaround, for a model operation?

The place to start is by saying: "We are going to open our Branch

University on X date." Make the commitment. Once you do that, you will get people excited and the whole development process takes on an enhanced urgency and relevance.

To answer the questions of (i) who needs what? and (ii) where do I get my faculty?, I recommend drawing a Branch Productivity Curve (BP Curve). What the BP Curve shows is the cumulative performance of your field locations.

Performance is defined by you – it could be defined by the last 12-months' profitability, change in profitability (increase or decrease over the prior 12 months), or whatever single metric is most important to your organization today. Once you've got a measurement, you stack rank the offices according to that measurement.

Once you've got a stack ranking, you chart branch performance cumulatively. You can do this for five locations or 25,000. For the sake of simplicity, in the chart below we will chart 50 branches as an example. The first dot on the far left is the performance of the # 1 highest-performing location in Company X. The second dot is the combined performance of location #s 1 and 2. The third dot is the combined performance of #s 1, 2 & 3. And so on, until we reach the farthest dot on the right, which is the combined performance of all 50 of Company X's field locations.

Branch Productivity Curve

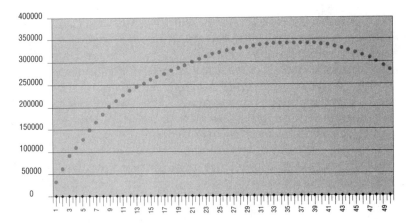

This curve will look different from every organization, but it tells you a couple things at a glance:

- The number of "speculative branches" you operate today. This is determined by drawing a line directly west from the farthest point on the east. Where that line intersects the BP Curve distinguishes between Income Properties and Speculative Properties. Speculative Properties are branches operating mostly for future promise as opposed to current results.

Income Producing vs. Speculative

Is this example, the number is 32. There are 50 total branches, and yet the top 18 are making as much money as the combined 50, so 32 branches are there mostly for future investment! The ratio of Speculative Branches to Income Properties is almost 2:1 (32:18).

Beyond determining the ratio of Speculative Branches to Income Properties, you can start to organize branches by contribution, not just regional geography[9]:

- **Income Properties** – the first 18 branches.
- **Spec Branches on the Bubble** – branches 19 thru 43. These are either marginally profitable or just breaking even. In the case of the marginally profitable, their profits are eaten up by the offices that are losing money.
- **Spec Branches Underwater** – branches 44 thru 50.

Income Properties should be the sources of Best Practices in all Projective Virtues (Discipline, Environment & Innovation), and should be coached on how to even more effectively capture their Innovation for their benefit and the benefit of the whole company.

Spec Branches on the Bubble should receive learning opportunities in the area of Discipline. Are the brand standards being adhered to? Is the sales process being executed consistently? What disciplined activities would lead to accelerated growth and internal case studies on "How to Become an Income Property"?

Spec Branches Underwater should be examined for Environmental compliance: are they hiring correctly, should we have a location there, is there something wrong with the site's design or upkeep, did we hire local management correctly, has adequate (i.e., company-standard) technology been installed? If an individual branch passes the Environment test, only then do we ask what disciplined activities would lead to a turnaround?

The actual metric can be determined according to your organization's current needs and culture. Some companies will use net profit, others will use profit growth, others will use something unique to their needs. But the key idea is that whatever you use is the most important thing to measure! And regardless of measurement, we owe it to the branches to let each branch know where they are on the BP Curve.

The Projective Virtues of Discipline and Environment are based on things you already know about your business. Or at a minimum, on things you can discover based on current data.

But what about Innovation? How do you most effectively work with your Income Properties to enhance their creativity? How does a company get better at developing scaleable new ideas? And how do you preserve cash flow while you are doing it – after all, you can't take your best people out of the field for very long or you'll lose productivity. The answer lies in the method one uses to create advantage…so why not use a proven method. The Scientific Method:

1. Observation(s)
2. Theory
3. Testing
4. Validation

To make observations, you have to have situational awareness. If you're observing creatively, you improve the chances for a meaningful outcome.

To develop meaningful theories, you need to be able to apply your intelligence to problem-solving. You have to provide a possible solution, not just identify the problem.

To test, you need a plan, commitment and a control group.

To validate, you need patience!

Nanobranch Labs...Using the Scientific Method to Create, Test & Replicate New Ideas in Your Branches

The articulation of the four steps shown above will vary by industry and footprint. For example, the starting Observation may be unique to your business. It may involve revenue, customer count, quality or a certain line item expense. But as much as the articulation varies, the method should not.

How do you begin to apply the rigors of this method to your branch issues? You've already started. You understand the six virtues of high-performing branches and together we have discovered how we can achieve all six virtues by focusing on the right three (Discipline, Environment & Innovation). In subsequent chapters, we will hear a dozen real-world branch experts describe how they create improvements in each of the three Projective Virtues. Understanding this material will improve the quality of the Observations and Theories within your business.

This book started with the very general and is now moving to the very specific. It began with the common ground for all branch-based businesses (growing same-store sales, improving quality, enhancing the brand). It then examined the most frequently cited obstacles to growth (the Periodic Table of Branch Vices). Next it advanced to an understanding of the Six Virtues in which three were the true drivers for top-performing locations.

Now it's time to consider the best way to capture the unique opportunities resident in your marketplace and through your operations. This is what leaders do. They start by building a solid foundation and then create something distinctly attractive on top of that foundation. By attractive, I mean something that magnetically attracts customers and employees to your business.

The best people to exercise highly individualized creativity are those employees, customers and other stakeholders in your organization today. We won't attempt to give you your next product, service or process – but we can learn from the best organizations what methodology works best when composing great ideas. We call this process **nanobranchology**.

Nanobranchology is the application of the Scientific Method to fundamental issues within the branch Environment. It is the scientific study of <u>elementary</u> branch problems – the tiny, "subatomic" activities that make or break the complex operating Environment of the branch. In a funny way, business is kind of like marriage: it's the small things that usually get you in trouble! The reason so many businesses fail to Innovate in a meaningful way is they attempt Innovation on a huge scale, instead of addressing the fundamental building blocks in their organization – that's how the treasury gets spent on the wrong acquisition, or ill-timed expansion. It's why they get stuck in a rut. And it's why creeping commoditization takes over the customer experience, the pricing, and the culture in so many organizations.

When we asked branch professionals why their Environment felt stale and commoditized at times – why new ideas failed to gain traction, here is what they told us…

"There are no new ideas here."
"There are too many new ideas here – it's Flavor of the Month."
"These so-called 'new ideas' are stupid – they have no impact on my business."
"No one asked the field for any input."
"No one spent the time up-front considering whether corporate could support this."
"No one spent the time up-front integrating this into our systems – now we're playing catch-up and doing double entry."
"The team responsible for implementation kept changing."
"No executive sponsorship."

Contrast those comments with the following model behavior. Behavior that addresses incremental change in a scientific way. And that doesn't seem techie or complicated. It's nanobranchology at work…

"What's in the Green Box for your Business?"

It's 7:00 a.m. The fifth of the month. President Pete walks into his office and begins to review today's To-Do-List. Preliminary financials for the prior period have just arrived. Forecast and Actual numbers look to be pretty close, but both are a bit short of Budget on the top line. Sales hiring and training is on schedule – but sales production is lagging. Pete has three customer visits and a board meeting scheduled for later this week. Employee turnover figures look to be a tad higher than expected.

At 7:04 a.m., this day becomes different from many of the days preceding it. The difference begins with a knock on the door.

It's one of the Vice Presidents with a small green box in her hand. "Good morning Pete, I have an idea which I think will improve the business and I'd like to test it. Do you have five minutes?"

"Sure," Pete replied.

"Great - thanks. Something came to my attention that you may be interested in. While reviewing our sales call activity, I observed that the Income Properties are generating 18% more sales calls per rep than the Speculative branches - and 40% more new account activity. When I compared the feet-on-the-street activity behind these results, I discovered one possible explanation for this difference. The sales reps in the Income Properties have been sending the prospect/customer something unique, an example of which I hold in this green box, after each and every face-to-face contact.

Now I'm not sure if I'm right. But I have a theory. I think the contents of this green box are contributing to the Income Properties' success in setting appointments and converting new accounts. I'd like to integrate this approach into the activity of ten of our Speculative Branches on the Bubble, over the next 90 days, and if I'm right, we will accomplish the following:

1. *Those participating Spec Branches on the Bubble will increase prospect/customer face time by 18%.*
2. *Those participating Spec Branches on the Bubble will increase new account activity by 40%.*
3. *It will cost "x" dollars and time to try this.*
4. *If we are right, the resulting increase in new account activity will generate "x" gross margin dollars and close the current gap to Budget.*

During the next 90 days, my administrator will monitor the results of this experiment. If it works the way I think it will, we will expand participation to a larger group of Spec Branches and validate our findings. That will let us know whether this is something worth establishing as a sales standard across the board. If we are right, I think we will generate an additional million dollars in revenue over "x" period of time by replicating this practice.

Now, at 7:09 a.m., President Pete had three immediate and simultaneous reactions to his VP's brief presentation. One, he wondered what the hell was in that green box and asked to see it. Two, he thought the theory made sense but wanted to see it played out before committing the entire organization to it. Three - and by far most importantly, he realized that if he had five people who thought like this VP, he could make his organization far more disciplined and competitive. Central to this realization was the idea that whatever was in the box was far less important than the fact that the VP logically identified its contents as a change agent...and had a plan for testing her theory.

How many times in your career has an employee knocked on your door and said <u>specifically</u>, "Boss, I've noticed something happening (Observation) and I've got an idea (Theory) that I think will generate "x" million dollars in additional revenue. Take a look at this…"

Let's put ego aside and admit to the fact that there are more million-dollar ideas in the brain cells of our workforce than there are in our single heads, regardless of how smart or attuned to the business we are. Consider the alternative: where the president always knows more about the opportunities for his company than his entire workforce knows as a collective unit. That egghead-Humpty-Dumpty-president has done a very poor job of hiring and development.

As leaders of companies, of business units, of branches, of departments, there are a few simple steps we can take to get more of our people thinking like the VP in the story above.

The reason the VP's presentation was so effective was <u>not</u> due to wordsmithing. And it was <u>not</u> due to political savvy. At this point, we don't even know what is in the box, so we <u>cannot</u> say that the individual idea has merit. But the process used to develop and test that idea felt good for a reason: it was rooted in the time-proven Scientific Method.

Good as it sounded, the Green Box experiment described above will not change the company's future so dramatically as to allow everyone involved to retire as millionaires. Mastering the process just might. That simple process is what you want to train your Income Properties how to master. That's Innovation 101 – the process not the idea.

Summary Framework to Improve Branch Performance

I didn't want to start with the framework because it's easy to get hung up on "where we are" instead of understanding what model branch behavior looks like. But after covering the Periodic Table of Branch Vices, the Six Virtues of High-Performance, and introducing the idea of a Branch University, the reader may be interested in where to start.

The process I personally use varies with the individual goals of each branch organization, but the framework is generally the same. Any or all of these four steps in the process shown below can be administered through your Branch University. There is usually some combination of internal development coupled with external resources (in other words, you don't need to write the entire curriculum yourself).

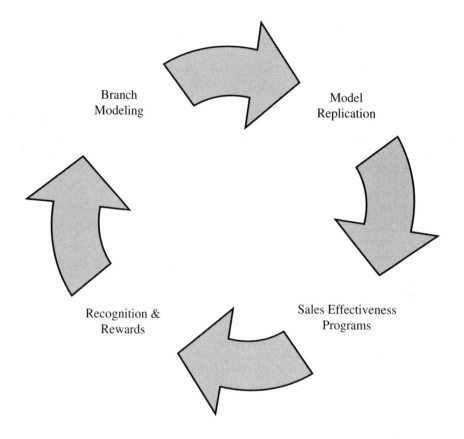

An expanded description of each of the cycle points is shown below.

Branch Modeling
- Differentiation Exercise (top 5% vs. middle 5% vs. corporate expectations)
- Documentation of Virtues & Vices
- Branch Productivity Curve
  - identify income-producers vs. speculative branches
  - capture best-practices of income-producers
  - target resources for spec branches on-the-bubble and spec branches underwater
- 90-Day Action Planning

Model Replication
- Financial Acumen (Financial Trust)
- Employee Development & Team Building (Cohesive Local Team)
- New Product or Service Workshops (Competitive Threat)

Sales Effectiveness Programs (I personally use the Miller Heiman

programs)
- Sales Training
- Customer Relationship Strategy

Recognition & Rewards[10]
- BranchFutures™ (pat. pend.)

If you seek improved field performance on a local and enterprise level, this summary framework is the place to start. An expanded application of these ideas is addressed in a seven-stage format in the final chapter ("Branching Out: From Idea to Execution").

Section II: Achieving the Projective Virtues

Discipline

Environment

Innovation

Discipline

Branch Training & Certification:
Sam Reese (CEO, Miller Heiman)
Damon Jones (COO, Miller Heiman)

Recognition & Rewards:
Stephanie LaPlace (EVP, 3PR Corporation)

Making & Managing Global Commitments:
Diane McIlree (Executive Manager, Spherion)

Regulatory Compliance by Branches:
Lawrence W. Marquess (Managing Shareholder, Litter Mendelson)

Training & Certification for Branches

What would you like to most change about your business today?

If you wanted to train your people to make that change – in the shortest period of time and at the least expense – how would you do it? Maybe you'd start by asking an expert...

The gentlemen interviewed for this chapter work for a company that has trained over one million people. Think about that number for a second. Now consider the fact that the words "training" and its more fashionable

---

This chapter was written in cooperation with Sam Reese and Damon Jones, both of Miller Heiman, Inc., a global sales consulting firm and a pioneer in the area of sales process training and reinforcement.

Sam Reese is the President & CEO of Miller Heiman. Prior to assuming that position, he was responsible for a staff of 1400 sales people at Corporate Express. Prior to that, Sam directed the commercial sales efforts of Kinko's Inc. as the VP of Sales. He personally led the growth of the commercial side from zero to $300 million per year; salesperson productivity more than doubled and average account billing increased fivefold.

Damon Jones is the COO of Miller Heiman. Prior to this role, he led the U.K. and European sales/operations efforts for Miller Heiman. He was introduced to the company's practices while serving at Guardian Royal Exchange Assurance - his training and employee development programs there led to a doubling of company revenue.

---

counterpart "learning" don't appear anywhere in the materials publicly describing their company. Instead they speak to the goals their clients seek through training. Why? Because training is a means to an end. And the end goal is more important than the box that gets checked saying, "We trained our new employees."

Some people think "great training" will push teams to "better results." But for training to work, the momentum has to come from the other direction. It has to be a pull, not a push. Excellent training makes the objective clearer - it takes the mystery out of success, pulling its audience into agreement and execution. It never clouds the objective - it clarifies and helps personalize the objective.

When I train, I don't want people to say, "Wow that was great training." That's not enough. Instead, I want people to say, "I now want to do my job in a different way." I personally don't want an evaluation of the facilitator as much as I want an evaluation of the participant: "What is the participant going to do differently?" Prove it.

I don't want to hear the words, "Great speech." Instead, I want to hear, "Let's go sack Carthage!" And then I want to see them go do it.

Before you can see them "go do it," you have to create change in a person's mind that will survive the journey back from the classroom to their branch. You have to start with an understanding of the way your people look at their branches. To the local people, "a branch is your own business…but it's not your own business." It's a balance of Innovation and Discipline - it's not one or the other. It's combining a proven operating framework with local creativity in execution. What does it look like when a branch deviates from the proven operating framework? Here's one example:

When the regional manager of a large well-known business services company visited a local retail operation, he noticed a part of the store cordoned off and prominently labeled the "Correction Connection." What did that mean? A close examination of the products there revealed a business within a business: one designed to serve the needs of visitors to the local prison!

Now, while the local store manager's initiative and creativity might be admired, he was having trouble understanding why the business-to-business trade in his establishment was lagging behind his peers. Do you think it had anything to do with what his local experiment was communicating!? That business customers were waiting in line with people on their way to the penitentiary? Why not promote a greeting card line called Friends of Felons!!

Incremental sales are great, but not if they cloud the positioning of your brand. In this example, the primary focus was supposed to be on the business customer (who spent hundreds or thousands of dollars a year) not the occasional walk-in who needed a "Spring has Sprung...Hope You'll be Sprung Too" card.

The operating framework cannot be established without a training strategy. And a training strategy requires an:

- Identification of Need
- Design Plan
- Delivery Plan
- Assessment Plan

When people are trained under a solid operating platform, every project and every meeting can start with a purpose, a time-frame and an intent. The platform provides standard operating procedures, but it also provides something else: a very good control mechanism to tell you who is on the team. People will rarely come right out and <u>say</u>, "I'm about half-committed here." But their compliance (or noncompliance) with the platform <u>will</u> speak to their commitment: that's how the establishment of a common operating platform can operate as a control mechanism.

If the platform is neglected, so is the underlying business. If the field management isn't asking the same questions around the same objectives, you lose the one advantage of multiple locations: leveraging what works and working toward common replication.

Unfortunately, many field managers will ask some questions repetitively, but use the wrong ones:

"How ya' doin'?"
"Who's the new guy over there?"
"Did you hear what those idiots at corporate are trying to do? Don't listen to them – listen to me: I'm the man!"
"Where's happy hour tonight?"
"How do I get back to the airport again? See ya' in 6 months!"

Getting from ad hoc management to scaleable management requires a unifying influence.

One highly effective unifying influence (the thing that keeps the so-called experts and immature field managers from running a "flavor-of-the-month" education campaign) is establishing a common language and process around your brand standards. And local mentoring is never enough to drive this common language and process. **Even the best field managers need some support from the corporate office around company standards.**

Consider the impact of no common language and process:

A new regional manager invites his district managers to report on key customers and the overall operating results. Now, everyone invited knew that there were some things that were important to all the districts represented:

Profits
Revenue Growth
Controlling Expenses
Increasing Customer Count
Improving Customer Retention through Quality Initiatives

But the district managers were not used to consistently giving the same type of report back to the company. So the outcome was:

Several managers gave excellent presentations.
Some had to be taken aside and asked to completely re-tool their presentations.
Some managers focused on profitability.
Some managers focused on profit growth.
Some managers used PowerPoint.
Some managers used Word.
Some managers used Excel.
Some managers talked about last week's key sales events.
Some managers talked about which people needed to be trained or replaced.

After 30 minutes in each presentation, the regional manager had either learned everything – or learned nothing.

At the end of Day One, the new regional manager saw the benefit to a common language and reporting system. More importantly, he realized that without some standard communication expectations in place, he could not adequately roll up the message he had heard and make recommendations to corporate that would be meaningful in their application for customers. And this was only one meeting! What would the confusion factor look like if the regional manager was comparing the content of the last four times these people got together?

If the only thing that is consistent between meetings is that (i) travel is involved, (ii) there is a cocktail hour after everyone is done, and (iii) the presenters are nervous beforehand and relieved afterward, those are the memories an organization is institutionalizing. What an opportunity for improvement and differentiation for this regional manager – and he took it!

By agreeing on three or four key metrics and fulfilling them, managers can simplify the process by which they help their people achieve success. Without these common goals, it's like talking to parents who believe their kids are brilliant even thought they keep bringing home "Fs". Johnny's so smart that he's bored = our people are great, but we're different out here than in the other markets.

Sure you are. You are different in the respect that you are making less money than the other districts. Just saying you are different is a way of asking for more time and passively waiting for something to happen. The only difference that matters is that you are acquiring the right kinds of customers, and growing profits, faster than your peers – that is the type of difference that matters.

That's a difference in execution not in market conditions. And here is how execution is linked to training: the right kind of training for most companies is execution-based, rather than strategy-based. If your strategy is so complicated that it requires training, you probably need to rethink your strategy. Think about it from your customers' perspective: they want to quickly understand why they are doing business with you. They want to see service consistency. They want you to take something that is potentially complicated and simplify it for them.

The proper role of training in all this: help your people understand the steps involved in execution so that their performance seems smooth to the customer/observer. There is zero benefit to a distributed network of personnel if they all are confused about how the machine is supposed to work and which activities matter in their positions.

Now, there are some companies that train simply to "keep everybody happy." But in the end, what really makes the important people (your customers and employees) happy is a focus on results, not just happiness. If happiness is the reflective quality, smart training can be the projective counterpart.

Why Training Sometimes Fails to Stick

When managed like an event, or used like an assembly line designed for repetitive tasks, training acquires the reputation of something you have to endure. By focusing on current business problems or objectives, training becomes problem-solving, which is far more engaging.

Think about the training "events" that you have participated in. Did they train you to think? Or were they merely festivals of regurgitation?

Now there is a huge trend in training today and that is Certification. Naming individuals within the training organization that are certified as experts in the field for which they are responsible. The force behind this trend is the universal belief that each of our businesses is completely unique, but might benefit from some lessons learned in other companies – provided they are tailored to the local situation. We're trying to grow top-line revenue, or improve quality, or enhance the brand – but our needs are so special that we're unlikely to benefit from training that actually worked somewhere else.

Maybe that's right. Maybe it isn't. On the surface is a kernel of truth, but there are a couple of caveats.

1. The credibility of delivery is key. Just because someone inside the organization says they are an expert does not mean they will be perceived that way by people whose livelihood depends on the training.

2. A trainer cannot remain in that position full-time without losing credibility. Rotation into production roles is critical to maintaining credibility.

Where certification works, it is accompanied by a tight model for expectations around competencies that you need: "This is what you have to be good at. Our model is proven enough that we feel good about developing trainees to execute these specific tasks – they will change the outcome here." If you're not 100% sure about this assertion, you cannot make money with your training. Developing skills that unquestionably make money for the company and the individual are core to training that sticks.

Another challenge in training is that it's become extremely accelerated. Where it used to take weeks to train an operator to achieve literacy on a company's technology, the expectation today is that it should take (literally) minutes or hours. The attention span of the trainee has shortened considerably over the past decade. This observation has led many responsible for skills development to figure that a five-day program could really be accomplished in five hours.

This impatience sometimes manifests itself in an attitude of wait-and-see. "We believe in training, but not at the expense of productivity." "We'll do training during the slow season." Believe that and you ensure you will have a slow season. And your trainees will view the training as a <u>medicine</u> instead of a <u>vitamin</u>. As a one-time fix instead of continuous learning. How do you improve your chances? First, by moving beyond training as an event.

One company I spoke with liked to allocate training funds (developmental assets) in the following way:

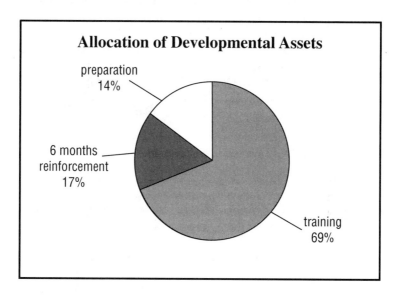

Simply by formally scheduling pre- and post-training activities, this model improves idea retention and employee retention – while actually reducing training expense.

How do your people prepare for classroom time? How do your people reinforce what was learned in the classroom? What are the right numbers for your company? Should training be developed internally, externally, or both?

Inside vs. Outside

If you have this choice available, you can take action confidently once you've answered the following questions for your company:

• How happy am I with my current training platform?
• Can I predict the outcome and measure the expense per person?
• What resources are available internally vs. externally?
• What expertise do we need relative to content?
• What expertise do we need relative to delivery?
• How long can we afford to wait for implementation?
• How will we benchmark whether this training is any good?
• Are we naming trainers for political reasons or for proven skill sets?

- If the person designing the training leaves the company mid-stream, how will that set us back?
- How long can I afford to take highly productive people out of the field for their new role as trainers?
- How will we train our trainers?
- Can we address the credibility gap faster by combining internal and external resources?

The answers will come out differently for every company, but there is one universal truth: the worst approach is to use trainers (inside or out!) who are not experts in their field. Lots of people feel like they can train. But there is a science to it. The best way to keep your analysis scientific is to refer back to the four-point systematic training cycle:

1. Identify the Need

This is often bypassed in the rush to get started or make a change, but is critically important. Is there a knowledge gap? A skill gap? A behavioral gap? How do those gaps tie to business performance objectives?

Are knowledge, skill and behavioral requirements clearly stated in job descriptions and performance reviews? Is training really the solution to our problem or is there a different issue, say hiring or compensation?

How important is training to the organization? For example, what if the company announced that there would be no training for employees next year? Would that be well-received?

How is the business changing – and how can training be used to address those changes?

How truly unique is the need you identified? For example, reclaiming spent nuclear waste for a specific design of reactor is more unique than increasing customer count or identifying decision-makers in the sales process. If your organization's learning solution can be fast-tracked by using industry-proven rather than company-specific experience, there is a significant speed advantage to outsourcing the design and/or delivery phases (next).

2. Design the Training

Once the gaps have been identified in Step One, what are the best methods for closing those gaps? Classroom? On-line? Exercises? Method workshops?

Early in the 20th century, the U.S. Army determined that there was an optimum learning method for training someone how to fire a rifle for the first time. This method was used millions of times and forms the basis for much of our understanding of vocational training. The method involves 10% explanation, 25% demonstration and 65% observed practice. The U.S. Army wisely saw that you can't separate the person from the training. And it determined that this specific mix of learning styles was the most effective combination.

Does your training design integrate these three experiences for the trainee: explanation, demonstration and observed practice? For the type of training you need designed, which explanations, demonstrations or exercises can you purchase off-the-shelf?

Does this training address execution rather than strategy?

How is problem-solving integrated into each day's efforts?

3. Deliver/Implement

Where will the training take place? How long should it take? What size group is optimum for this type of training? Who will do the training[11]? Are the trainers perceived as experts? What is the optimum ratio of trainers to learners? How will the knowledge, skills and behaviors taught be linked back to performance? Are we only training on things that we can measure?

How much should we spend?

How do we define the role of the executive sponsor? Of the training provider? Of the participant?

What does successful delivery look like? How quickly can we expect to see results?

4. Evaluate/Review

It's not just about the classroom! How will we assess pre-training competency levels? How does one measure learning "in progress", that is as it takes place? How will we know whether the training stuck?

What are the right questions to ask when evaluating training? What are the right questions to ask when evaluating trainees? Who do you ask? Who asks the questions?

This is a real challenge, because there are myriad factors at work and very seldom do you get to establish control groups. Most companies simply aren't willing to say, "Let's not train 10% of the workforce and compare their results with the trained people."

This is one advantage of using an external resource. You can benchmark your progress post-training with that of other companies...and with that of your own organization prior to a specific training engagement.

In closing our consideration of these four factors, we'll go back to the army theory: you can't separate the person from the training. Will a certain type of training allow you to attract and retain a higher caliber person to your organization?

When you are setting up a Branch University within your company, take a lesson from the institutions most respected for their ability to develop people: they accelerate learning by avoiding the extremes. They don't rely completely on outsiders and they don't suffer from "Not Invented Here" disease. By balancing the needs of each incoming class with the resources available both internally and externally, they reduce cost and increase retention.

Recognition & Rewards

What is the best way to positively and consistently reinforce brand standards and objectives? While writing this book, we received an unsolicited note from Canyon Cassidy, an IT professional who helps us with technical issues in our own company. The note read, "Write about rewards and recognition!"

Of all the things he could have asked about, he was most interested in the way companies reward and recognize the special efforts of the people running the day-to-day operations. Is Canyon any different from the rest of us? Don't we all wonder, "Am I appreciated? Is what I'm doing making a difference here? Does anyone care?"

This chapter was written in collaboration with Stephanie LaPlace.

Ms. LaPlace is the Executive Vice President of 3PR Corporation. She advocates creative Recognition & Reward programs because they personally motivated her to quickly achieve success: she was named "Rookie of the Year – U.S. Operations" for her work in a startup operation for a global services firm.

In her subsequent work as a career consultant, the # 1 complaint she has heard, at the senior executive level and throughout the organizational hierarchy, is that good work often goes unrecognized. This chapter presents a unique framework which couples workforce motivation and reinvestment in the company.

Ms. LaPlace serves as a founding member of the Branch Productivity Institute's BPI Congress.

Let's start by looking at this issue from a historical perspective.

- Have you ever heard of a military organization that did not recognize courage in the field?

- Have you ever attended a school that didn't recognize its top performers?

- Can you name a culture that survives today that didn't recognize its best and brightest along the way?

- Do you remember, from your own childhood, being motivated by a blue ribbon or a trophy or a pat-on-the-back from a person you respected?

Bottom line: people need to be recognized in a way that is meaningful to them. That recognition is what keeps them engaged. If they don't get it in your workplace, they'll seek it someplace else. The best people hunger for alternative sources of Recognition & Rewards ("R&R") if they don't get it from you.

Now, every company in America claims it has the best people and no one wants to believe they have the worst! After all, when is the last time you can remember a CEO publicly stating, "The people really don't matter"? It just doesn't happen (in public, anyway[12]).

These self-congratulatory claims to possessing the best people usually ring hollow with the real "best people." Why? Because by definition not every company can have the best people. What makes you think you do? Can you prove it?

Here's a reality check: if an organization is not the most profitable business in its sector, what makes it think it has the best people? If a company isn't growing market share faster than its competitors, what makes it think it has the best people? If a team isn't winning, how can it say it is made up of winners?

It is disingenuous to say, "We have the best people...but we have average products, ordinary service standards, adequate infrastructure and marginal profitability or growth." That's hallucination, not observation.

So...why would the best people choose to work for your organization today?

Is it the money?

Is it security?

Is it the challenge or opportunity for promotion?

Is it because they will learn something at your company?

Why does it matter?

The # 1 SG&A expenditure for most branch and store based businesses is...personnel expense. Companies invest significant resources in the hiring, development and management of their respective workforces. And every company seeks to define its unique position in its market through its people. <u>One threshold question</u> is how much of R&R should be left to the discretion of individual managers - and how much should be defined within an overall platform of recognition.

For purposes of brand consistency and a uniform commitment to quality, the best approach is to standardize R&R. Why? Because a standardized approach is easier to measure, can be leveraged cost-effectively, and is less subject to individual whims and blind spots. Your overall goal in developing an internal program should be to create and sustain something that gives your company a unique, competitive advantage within its industry. A consistent internal program has an additional advantage: it makes selective recognition outside of the program feel like something special.

Organizations competing on more than just price seek market advantage via product offerings (best products and selection), customer relations (best service) and employee loyalty (best people). Why shouldn't the R&R program be held to this same standard - that of being the best?

The starting point is to make the commitment to develop an R&R program that is really the best - one that outsiders would love to emulate, if they only could! One that employees cite as a major reason for staying with the organization. How does one do that? There are entire consulting practices built around this topic. But one can get started by considering four factors within his or her organization:

1. Why?
2. What?
3. Who?
4. How?

Let's get started in our examination of these four factors.

> **Why?**
> What?
> Who?
> How?

• To retain your best employees, who in turn retain your best customers.

• To keep your intellectual property from walking out the door.

• To create a culture that feeds the Projective Virtue of Innovation and to have a measurably competitive spirit.

• To operate <u>more</u> cost-effectively....What? Don't reward programs cost money? No, they save you money. What costs you money is seeing your best people walk out the door with your best customers. What would you rather spend money on:

Advertising for new employees and new customers?		Cost-effective retention plans that also motivate greater productivity?
Introductory training for new employees (which as a group represent your highest turnover category)?		Continuous education for experienced employees seeking additional learning opportunities?
Higher employee benefits costs, especially in the area of health insurance?	**...or...**	Promoting work/life balance through incremental funding of employee health improvement?
Higher workers' compensation premiums?		Recognition programs which reward improvements in employee workplace safety.
Attorneys' fees for enforcing non-competes, non-solicitation agreements and invention clauses?		An internal royalties program that encourages Innovation?

A final note on cost-effectiveness: if your R&R program is not yet **self-funding** (meaning its impact on the bottom line exceeds its costs), that's a great opportunity to start over!

Earlier in Stephanie's career, while working for a B2B service company with global operations, she accepted the challenge to grow top line revenue for nine branches in the Chicago area. When she started in this particular market, thousands of miles from headquarters, the company had virtually zero name recognition. With 200 local competitors each operating an active local sales force, she couldn't advertise enough to cut through all the clutter. So she had to do something different.

The strategy: (1) hire the right people meeting fixed, proven criteria, (2) ensure that national, regional and local goals are in alignment, and (3) constantly review, reward and recognize local achievement in three tiers: nationally, regionally, and locally.

The result: Despite the initial lack of name recognition, the area enjoyed seven consecutive years of growth in the number of branches, revenue and profits. All within a highly competitive industry where everybody and their dog wanted the same business she did.

Built into the strategic plan was an organizational model that rewarded offices for reaching milestones in revenues and profit. Milestone by milestone, the sales organization and its management team reached their goals, increased market share, and improved name recognition. Local representatives' achievements were honored and recognized at two special sales conferences in the South Seas and Europe.

Realizing the importance of each employee and their integral part in achieving company goals, Stephanie built on the company's plan, expanding the rewards and recognition program to reach the non-management ranks at both the branch and area levels. As a result, the highly competitive Chicago area had virtually no turnover and posted record setting sales and profits under her leadership as Area Vice President.

Why do rewards and recognition matter within your organization?

What greater goal do you seek by offering additional incentives?

Are you trying to solve structural issues or motivational issues with your R&R?

Every organization has its own unique objectives, but there are three fundamental goals that any organization can use as its starting point. They are...

1. Increasing same store sales.
2. Improving quality (or reducing waste).
3. Improving the brand.

These goals are inextricably linked with financial reliability, team cohesion and competitive power: the <u>Reflective Virtues</u>. Why reward these things? Why not!

Why?
What?
Who?
How?

What should you recognize and reward?

Recognize the **activities** that increase same-store sales, improve quality (or reduce waste) and positively differentiate your brand. Those activities represent the Model Behavior for your organization today. Reward measurable **results.**

What are you rewarding? Top line growth? Service capacity utilization? Customer loyalty and account penetration? New account sales? Employee creativity? Increased customer traffic during non-peak operating periods? What changes in your business would really make your business look different at the end of the reward cycle?

Would greater Discipline within your brand standards lead to greater profitability? Then focus on compliance with those standards.

Does the company need new brand standards (or new product/service offerings) to remain competitive or keep margins healthy? Then applaud Innovation.

What would you say is the greatest single difference in behavior between your top-performing field locations and the merely average field locations? Recognize the adoption of that different (model) behavior where it occurs!

When considering what motivates your workforce to adopt model behavior – and consequently deliver improved results – it makes sense to start with two categories: input & output. Behavior and Results. Activity and Impact. Projective Virtues and Reflective Virtues! As a leader, one of the most important things required of you is to make sure that the

Activity you choose to reward actually yields the Result desired. That there is a real nexus between Activity & Result: start with the Result desired and then work backwards to determine the activities most likely to generate that result.

Let's take the goal of increased sales as an example. What measurable activities are worth recognizing?

Measurable Activity	Considerations
1) Viable Target List or Prospect Database Created	Leads to more time spent on the right types of prospects.
2) Number of Qualified Appointments with new prospects	Measures the ability and persistence of your sales force.
3) Documentation in System	Allows quicker access to customer records by the service team.
4) Number of Anniversary Visits to Existing Clients	Reminds customers of your past service and experience with their account.
5) Number of Referrals Obtained	Shortens the sales cycle and reduces skepticism on the part of new prospects.
6) Number of Follow Up Activities	Encourages more than casual relationships with the prospect pool.
7) Number of Service Calls or Office Tours	Expands the Home Field Advantage.
8) Number of Prospecting Calls	Increases introductory activity in the sales process.
9) Number of salespeople hired	Who else is going to do the other nine things on this list!
10) Management Introductions	Improves depth of customer relationships.

So much for activities. What results might you reward and in what way?

Result Sought	Reward in what way?
Human Resources – reward good hires	Training allocation for new employees that meet ALL hiring criteria.
Attendance and/or longevity	Gift for spouse or family.
Better intelligence on competitors	Corporate provides targeted intelligence for your market at its expense.
Sales – increased customer count (via new account activity), increased sales per customer, better account penetration (especially through branch cross-selling)	Beyond the commission plan, access to improved leads or administrative support.
Customer care	Appoint top-performers to the faculty of your Branch University.
Reduced Days Sales Outstanding, Improved Collections	Your customers pay quicker, corporate provides enhanced A/R services to your branch.
Manufacturing production	Employee or site featured in marketing material.
Safety	Corporate subsidizes the cost of safety equipment for your branch's employees.
Reduced errors/Improved Quality	Replace boxy monitors with flat-screens for employees with quality contributions.
Problem-solving	Leadership roles available on Best Practice Campaigns within your Branch University!
Innovation – new products or services	Internal royalty program.

The great thing about any R&R program is it puts you in the driver's seat. Instead of reacting purely to financial demands and staff needs, you get to say <u>what</u> you are willing to pay for.

Why?
What?
Who?
How?

Who should you recognize and reward? Well there's a simple three-step process to answer this question.

Step One:

You should only R&R those people that have some ability to impact the success of your organization. So start by making a list of the people that can have absolutely no impact on your organization's success.

OK, got that list? Fire them. Why would you have someone on the payroll that can have absolutely no impact on your organization's success!

Step Two:

Now that you've stopped paying people who can have absolutely zero impact on your company's success, that leaves the people who are actually important to you.

Within this population (the people who can make or save you money), write down the names of the people who need zero recognition, who would work for free, who don't ever need to be told they're part of the team, who are so committed to you that you could ignore them for twenty years and they would still lay their life on the line for you.

OK, got that list? Fire them too.

Why!!! Because they are either robots, androids, or communist spies. Whatever they are, there is something wrong with them. "Best people" don't commonly accept suffering as part of their payment. You are not the Messiah. You are not that motivational. You are not that good! So get rid of the phonies that pretend they enjoy being ignored...they're probably stealing from you!!

Step Three:

Who's left? Everybody else. Everybody else needs to be recognized for his or her contributions. The hallmark of strong leadership is to understand the degree of impact different people can have. And then to recognize impact appropriately.

The employee most passionate about the company's success.
The receptionist ("Director of First Impressions").
The top salesperson.
The salespeople with the best current growth ("Most Improved").
The accounts receivable/collector with the best stats.
The help-desk person who goes out of their way to actually help.
The shipping and receiving guys.
The most tenured employee.
The newest employee.
Your marketing team.
The person with the new idea.
Employees at corporate.

Bottom line, if you've got 1000 employees with an average IQ of 100 each, your collective organizational IQ could be 100,000! Don't reduce the collective IQ of your workforce by ignoring 30% of the team.

What about <u>outside</u> the workforce?

Do you recognize...

Vendor performance? Channel contributions? Customer loyalty? Community contribution to your company's success? Board members that contribute sales leads? Employees' kids that do something great? (A $500 scholarship and certificate here might be worth more than a $5000 employee bonus check.) Employees' spouses? (Especially when the employee has perfect attendance.)

The organization depends on everyone that touches it – this interdependency is why the word "organization" shares the same root as the word "organism." If you have a toothache, your whole body feels it. If just one part of the organization is sick or underperforming, everyone is impacted. So who should you recognize? Anyone that can have an impact on the success of your organization: that's who!

Why?
What?
Who?
How?

<u>How</u> can you best recognize and reward contributions? What frequency makes the most sense? What role should corporate play? How about the role of the region or the local management?

Consider the programs you've experienced in your career and make those experiences work for you and your team. What recognition or reward in your career seemed to have the greatest impact on you personally? Have you experienced any R&R that demotivated you or your team?

The <u>how</u> matters. It can range from formal (i.e., a plaque) to informal (integrating meaningful recognition into weekly meetings). From an expensive trip to a simple thank-you note. The how may be configured as an expense or a reinvestment.

Some of us have been on series of trips celebrating some success in a given period. Those junkets cost the company a lot of money...some are remembered and some are forgotten. In contrast, being invited to corporate to brainstorm changes or work on a pilot program that could impact the whole organization – that trip is remembered forever, especially if your idea is adopted throughout the company.

I've visited branch offices where <u>awards from ten years ago</u> still hung as testaments to a job well done. The sad thing about a couple of those trips is that those offices went unrecognized for ten years, despite their ongoing top production: someone got lazy about recognizing top performance (it's kind of like seeing an Employee of the Month plaque posted where the last entry is two years old!).

On the flip side, I still remember visiting a corporate office where I saw nothing in the lobby but photos of employees who made that company successful. Now that company[13] constantly reinforced the importance of its people's contributions: you couldn't get through the front door without seeing the importance they attached to employee recognition.

Reinvestment = Win/Win

No matter which program you select for your organization, the Return on Investment can be maximized – and the risk of the program minimized – by channeling Reward dollars toward purchases that benefit both the individual honoree and the company.

For example, if you are prepared to spend $3,000 per winner, why not invest that money in a special Client Event that will make the winner look like a hero (as opposed to sending the winner $3,000 and having him or her blow it in Vegas, baby).

Why not consider an R&R methodology where the money stays inside the company? One example is a unique R&R program called BranchFutures™ (pat. pend.), which was developed at 3PR. Its seven-step process assigns "market-values" to certain key activities and results – and rewards performance while reinvesting in personal and company growth.

It's not enough for the company alone to win – the honored employee has to see that the additional investment made on his or her behalf (the "reward") is also boosting their own individual performance and status within the company. It's like saying to a basketball team, "You've got the best record, therefore you get Home Field Advantage in the finals." Winning an extra edge is what motivates an elite class to perform at even higher levels.

Making & Managing Global Commitments

Do we want global customers? Why?

- Increased revenue and cash flow
- Increased predictability in forecasting
- Large, household name accounts can be used as quality-provers to the remainder of the marketplace…if they don't destroy your profitability in the meantime!
- Increased barriers to entry for competitors in your accounts
- Increased barriers to exit for some large customers

What does it take to sell and service more global customers? Why do global customers seek consolidation of services purchased? Does your field model provide the capacity and consistency required in today's metric-driven marketplace?

This chapter was written in cooperation with Diane McIlree.

Diane McIlree is a business development and relationship management professional with more than 20 years experience establishing and growing staffing relationships in multiple lines of business. Her experience encompasses early-stage through multi-billion dollar operations. Diane has been instrumental in growing relationships with Global Accounts across a variety of industries. Her experience extends to establishing new markets and product lines, in professional services, legal staffing and Information Technology.

Ms. McIlree serves as a founding member of the Branch Productivity Institute's BPI Congress.

The best place to start answering these questions is an examination of why global prospects seek to reduce the number of qualified suppliers…

- Lower cost through volume purchasing.
- Cost predictability.
- Standardize processes.
- Streamline operations.
- Control the "native language" – reducing the Tower of Babel syndrome where a plethora of vendors introduce confusion into measurement and execution.
- Enforce business rules through global relationships – e.g., one global investment bank wanted better control of project assignments: they wanted to avoid bringing in contractors for less than three days or more than 45 weeks.
- Outsource things that are not the buyer's core competence.
- Outsource things that are currently more cost-effectively procured through a third party.
- Reduce in-house staff dedicated to vendor management. One large financial services provider replaced its in-house department with a third party management service that coordinates their spend and quality control for 25 different vendors.
- Simplify the operating requirements: when a relationship gets close to evergreen, there is an opportunity for continuous improvement.
- Reduce the risk of renegade spend or departmental noncompliance.

One example of these goals in action involves one company's use of Accenture to act as a procurement pipeline. The consulting firm built channels for every major commodity of spend, vendor approval, order, analysis, and compliance of terms. Partners then hook into a dedicated SAP and all speak to common metrics. The result was reduced errors in the process and fewer, more streamlined global relationships.

With this type of service now in play at almost every global user, the way things are purchased is changing. How has the large account relationship evolved over the past five to seven years? First of all, it is no longer enough for the global supplier to focus solely on the core service that is their core competency: operational excellence is a given, just one price of admission. The global supplier now must also bring consultancy and replicable best practices. The client wants best-in-class experts in service administration, not just the core product or service purchased.

The threshold for this type of relationship might have been an annual spend of $50 million just a few years ago. It's closer to $10 million today...and dropping. And the trend suggests that while some smaller companies are happy today receiving good core products and services with simple billing, even those smaller companies' expectations will rise as they seek to achieve the efficiencies being modeled in larger organizations.

Who is driving this change? Is it the large buyer interested in compensating for their own shrinking margins? The sophisticated vendor seeking differentiation? The third party coordinator promising cost reductions? The corporate governance demands of the investment community and securities regulators? Yes, yes, yes and yes: it's really an intersection of all four. It happens quicker on an individual basis when a large consulting company is engaged to manage bidding. And the result there may be that the client uses more junior contacts to control the program...which may become a fatal flaw.

When there is only parenthetical interest in the program from a very high-level...on a spend that is seven or eight figures, it can start to look like dereliction of executive duty and a dumbing-down of a significant spend. One reason Diane McIlree's company, Spherion, has a 96.3% client satisfaction rate with its largest global account is that both parties have retained a high level of executive interest and commitment in execution: it's not just something you design, plug in and walk away from.

Where are the opportunities for efficiency leak? One is the bifurcated audience; multiple parties with different primary aims and the individual power to toss you out. If there is no solid integration between purchasing and the user groups, a split personality develops. This corporate schizophrenia is the result of inadequate executive sponsorship. The cure: high-level participation from design to execution to review.

Does a vendor need to be global to serve global customers? Not necessarily, but that vendor does need to be able to quickly adapt to the customer's level of infrastructure. An impossible task if there is disconnect between servicing offices or a lack of common standards from the get-go. These are not the accounts you want to use for "on-the-job training." You can't afford it: the pricing structure pushes the vendor to eat the cost of errors and remediation.

Are certain types of products and services more likely to be globalized? Yes. Core offerings that have been commoditized are looked at as no-brainer fit with this type of operating structure. One current challenge for the commodity provider is that, as demographics and Environmental factors change, what looks easy today may become quite costly and difficult to provide over the length of an extended contract. To the extent your product or service relies on raw materials, energy, personnel or other fluid supply sources, a hedge plan is required to ensure that you don't get burned downstream.

In a way, the large global relationship is like a futures contract: the purchaser seeks to enforce pricing consistency over the term of the contract and shift the cost burden of supply and compliance to the vendor…for as long as possible.

Another magnet for globalization in purchasing is the Bigger Spend. Buyers obviously care less about enforcing rules for the smallest line items on the P&L. And for good reason: the benefit is smaller. Finding a 4% increase in efficiency becomes more important when it is attached to a larger spend. And what are the three largest spends: personnel, technology and real estate.

So what happens next? When an organization like McKinsey & Company says, "We'll help you manage your supply spend," the logical response if you like their program is, "Why stop with our suppliers?" Why not move this control beyond suppliers and into organizational development? Or even into performance management?

Just a few years ago, 50 vendor relationships might have been managed by 50 to 100 internal managers. Today those managers may simply review the report of one independent third party. Today, every ten employees may be formally reviewed by a different manager. Is the next step to standardize performance reviews so that managers only respond to third-party benchmarking of their teams? Should it be?

If you believe the work process will continue to improve in efficiency, we may soon reach a point where companies can outsource the front-end management of new employees. On-boarding, dispatch of equipment, maybe the first 30 day performance review as well. Maybe even development, formatting of career path, all of personnel management except the sign-off.

Just about every Annual Report advances the theory that the Great Differentiator is "the people that work there." Is this a big lie? I mean, they can't all be right, can they? Can every company say it has the best people if it's not using some type of third party benchmarking? And the executives may be selling themselves short with this response. After all, you can hire the best people in the world and they won't stick around if you don't give them the right kind of leadership.

The opportunity that might seem Orwellian in scope, but could be coming: some companies today put a massive global systemization in place for just 5% of their workforce (the temporary employees, the project workers and the other contract service providers). If it works for them, what about the other 95%?

What about that other 95%? Are you as efficient as your industry peers in your workforce utilization today? How would you know that if you rely solely on local management review? You certainly can't tell solely by looking at personnel expense as a percentage of sales: sales includes too many other factors.

These next phases in this evolution will probably come from the same place as the last ones...the consulting industry, accompanied by a very small handful of progressive vendors. In the example of the $70 billion staffing industry, there was a notable dearth of thought leadership in the area of driving customer usage and efficiency: some strong exceptions to this rule know this because they managed to grow their top line and gross margin when everyone else has flat-lined or lost margin. But, by definition, not everyone is the exception. And just sayin' it don't make it so.

Many service providers continue to crank out 200 page proposals where the only page that matters is the price list (which is now closer to one sentence: "our markup is x% over cost"). Claiming thought leadership while operating in that manner is delusional, and represents a window of opportunity for the select few who can stop boring their prospects.

Why do prospects get bored? Is it because we're all alike? No. Just because you sell a perceived commodity does not mean your customers are not interested in saving more money on that commodity or improving delivery options. But dumbing-down is a source of boredom. If your customer is twice as smart as you are, when your business acumen lags that of the person you are calling upon, the customer gets bored pretty quickly. Think about an example from the largest sector in the largest geographic market in the U.S. The financial services industry in New York. The decision-maker you seek to influence is one of the most brilliant minds in the world. And you're going to have them face off with whom from your organization? Someone with big hair and "moxie" from a local branch office? Those days are gone.

That's just one scary example. Let's get out of New York City and visit the Midwest. For years, the $70 billion staffing industry could sell its services to the manufacturing and distribution sectors with far less understanding than their customer had of the sophisticated mechanics that go into any well-run production or distribution facility. The eager beaver sales guy pounds on a lot of doors, drops off donuts and adds value by lowering the rate rather than understanding the dynamics that affect safety, attendance, just-in-time delivery or any of the other challenges facing that customer. The customer is ten times smarter about his business than the person calling on him: and that is not the way to engage any prospect.

Think I'm exaggerating? How about logistical aptitude? In an industry that had some seven and eight figure write-offs for technology misadventures, there are still gaps in logistical aptitude. One large staffing company was just presented with a back-billing issue of $1.6 million from twelve months ago. Several times a year, we read of state and federal employment law violations from companies that are in the sole business of workforce supplementation. These are the kinds of mistakes that drive down price expectations from global accounts.

An industry that develops great skill in implementation, but does not anticipate future customers requirements, will restrict its customer's perspective to one where the customer dictates all the terms of the relationship.

How does the industry change this master/servant dynamic? It doesn't. But some individual companies have elevated their relationship to one of true partnership. They are in the minority. What would cause large, sophisticated, highly admired companies to look to a commoditized industry for real advice? Improved business acumen, a better understanding of the leading indicators important to service delivery. Preparation in making adjustments to demographic changes. Expertise in the process related to creating a global referral program, experience in managing a geographically diverse branch network, trends in offshoring, using technology to reduce the cost of hiring, performance cooperatives, channel partners vs. core staff.

Companies are willing to outsource these questions...they just haven't been presented with a compelling reason to do so with vendors who operate on a reactive, commodity basis.

The good news in these murky waters: a company that manages global relationships well can define its position in future markets. Obviously you can't just be a global thinker: your operational excellence has to be a given. But based on the earlier gaps outside of core delivery, a few smart, sound operators can build market share.

Where to start? Where the customer feels the most pain outside of the core offering. How is your reporting different? What advantage does your billing system provide? Would co-habitation in some of your field locations give the client a competitive opportunity? Could you "compete" with the client to improve performance in a key workforce metric...where you both win by improving attendance or productivity?

How do we re-engage the customer? Recapture the pioneering spirit that launched the business? Extend the thinking power of the industry beyond its own four walls? Improve the acumen of our own workforce?

Like any buying decision where you have two parties at the table, if one party is smarter, richer, and has a better infrastructure, what leverage is there for the other guy? That's a feudal system, not a partnership. That doesn't even rise to the level of a commodity: at least a commodity is highly predictable in some positive ways. It's just a low-priced, low-valued service.

The global relationships that endure will have to deliver more than just low prices and low-valued service. True partnerships in this arena will focus on Innovation and better anticipation of the underlying trends for both parties.

Regulatory Compliance by Branches

This chapter aims to arm the Branch or Store Manager with an understanding of the competitive advantage gained by complying with the many laws and regulations pertaining to his or her local business. One Branch Manager said it best...

"When I got my first job as a Branch Manager, the last thing I thought about was legal issues. I was focused on building the branch business and profitability. I thought, like many new Branch Managers, that 'legal problems only happen to other people.' I didn't really associate them with the branch finances. As I've grown more experienced, I've discovered that the failure to pay attention to the laws that apply to my business can seriously impact the business and its income statement."

This chapter was written in cooperation with Lawrence W. Marquess.

Mr. Marquess is the managing shareholder for the Denver office of Littler Mendelson, P.C., a national law firm representing management in labor and employment matters. He is a member of the Labor and Employment and Litigation Sections of the American Bar Association and a past Chairman of the Labor Law Committee of the Colorado Bar Association, 1989 - 1992.

One of the challenges endemic to operating in multiple markets is that the laws governing the business vary from market to market. And the starting point for the local manager is revenue not regulation: he or she wants to focus on attracting customers and building a profitable business. But it's not that simple: it's not just about revenue, but protecting your revenue from the cost of noncompliance.

Many of the laws that govern your business are federal laws, which do not vary from domestic market to domestic market. On the other hand, many day-to-day issues are governed not by federal law, but by state <u>or</u> local laws. Or they are governed by federal, state <u>and</u> local laws! Compliance with the laws applicable to your branch is, of course, further complicated by <u>changes</u> in the laws at the federal, state, and local levels. For example, in one recent 12-month period, the legislature in California passed three major revisions to the current employment and employee benefits laws. That, of course, reflects only one state.

So how does a company with multiple branches, and the managers of those branches, deal with the variety and the changes in the law?

You deal with it by being aware of the various types of laws that apply to your business and the variations of those laws from locality to locality. You determine at what level and who in your organization is going to be responsible for ensuring compliance, and then you train those responsible so that they know what the law is and how to maintain compliance. You also want to be sure that you have processes in place by which changes in the law are brought to the attention of those responsible for compliance.

If you are a branch or store manager, you may well ask, what has that got to do with me? The answer is that it has a lot to do with you as on-site management. It certainly has the potential for having a substantial impact on your part of the business. For example, think about the impact of a $250,000.00 judgment against the company, based on actions and activities of your branch, particularly if the cost of defending the lawsuit and the cost of the judgment are charged against your branch or store:

• A $250,000.00 judgment represents 5 million dollars in sales if you operate at a 5% return on sales.

• If the judgment comes in an action in which attorney fees are awarded to the prevailing party, the $100,000.00 in legal fees represents an additional 2 million dollars in sales at that 5% return.

- Additionally, the company will almost certainly have paid at least $100,000.00 in legal fees to defend the action, representing another 2 million dollars in sales.

- Depending on the nature of the case, the cost in attorney fees and damages awarded in a judgment may pale in comparison to the cost in time and energy to you and other employees in the branch as you answer discovery, undergo depositions, collect documents for production, and spend time talking to legal counsel.

- Moreover, if the claims are at all newsworthy, your branch or store's reputation may suffer from the publicity, not only after the judgment is announced, but also during the course of the proceedings.

- Moreover, the collateral damage can go on for years. Imagine, for example, the client or prospective client or lending institution that asks about your involvement and history in litigation. Sometimes, employees, customers, and boards of directors don't compartmentalize bad news. They may not remember that you prevailed, even if the result is publicized. They may only remember the initial negative publicity. Sometimes the question is, if you were wrong on this matter, what else have you screwed up?

Given all this, consider these two questions:

1. There are approximately 50,000 lawsuits filed every day in the United States. Would you rather focus on preventing lawsuits or fighting them?

2. If there are going to be a dozen major lawsuits in your industry in the next 12 months, how much more competitive can you be if those lawsuits are targeted at your competitors – and not at you and your store or branch?

The best way to avoid becoming a lawsuit target is to have a basic knowledge of the laws that apply to the part of the business for which you're responsible and take steps to comply with them. Know enough, at least, to know when a developing situation could create legal problems if it isn't handled properly, so that you can seek advice if you need it to stay within the law.

For example, consider these situations involving employment law, a common and fertile ground for legal problems for branch or store managers:

"Good Intentions – Bad Result"

Mark Maverick has been growing his branch faster than most. His marching orders from his Regional Vice President and from corporate have been simple: grow market share or die trying. Part of Mark's strategy has been to accept nothing less than superior performance from each of his branch employees. Mark is a classic "up by the bootstraps" kind of guy. His intentions are good - he wants to grow the business. He appreciates his employees and figures that what's good for the branch benefits them all.

In preparing for a new marketing campaign, Mark received approval to hire an administrative assistant. The administrative assistant's primary duties would be preparing mailers and quickly responding to inquiries from prospective customers. An important goal of the marketing campaign was to schedule each prospect for a meeting with the sales force within three days of receiving the inquiry. Mark interviewed several candidates and hired Carpel Carl, based on his experience and his references (one of which said Carpel Carl was so focused it was "almost like he had tunnel vision").

About two months into the job, Carpel Carl developed severe pains in his hands and wrists. It also became apparent that he was allergic to the ink in his computer printer. As a result, his production dropped by about 50%. It took him much longer to get out mailers, and as a result, he had less time to spend responding to calls. The allergies slowed him even more. As a result, it took him twice as long to respond to customer inquiries. Another consequence was that he began to miss several days of work each month for medical reasons.

When Mark noticed Carl's declining production, he gave him a warning : "Our customers expect better than a 5-day response time ... improve your performance or I'll have to let you go." Carl tried to explain his medical problems, but Mark held firm. Carl asked if he could use one of the clerks to help with the mailings, so that he would have more time to focus on responding to customers. He also told Mark that it would help if he could have a printer that didn't use the ink to which he was allergic.

Without even investigating to see if one of the clerks might have time to help, Mark told Carl that having someone else help him was out of the question. Mailings were Carl's job, and if he couldn't do them, Mark would have to hire someone who could. As to the printer, Mark said: I don't have a spare printer in this branch, and I don't have a new printer budgeted. He told Carl to do the best he could but warned that Carl was expected to meet the goals set for him when he was hired.

A month later Mark fired Carl because he wasn't meeting those goals. Two weeks after he was fired, Carl met with Jim Diamond, plaintiff's counsel extraordinaire, and two weeks later, Mark received notice that a charge of discrimination had been filed by Carl under the Americans With Disabilities Act with the United States Equal Employment Opportunity Commission

The charge eventually made its way into the federal court. A year after the charge was first filed, and after $75,000 in legal fees and costs and over a hundred hours of Mark's time in defending the matter, the case settled with a payment to Carl and his attorney of $100,000. The Company charged the legal fees and costs and settlement payments to Mark's branch. The charge ate his profits for the year and then some. Instead of being one of the most profitable branches, Mark's was one of the few substantial losers. Swept away also was Mark's bonus and any chance for a salary bump that year.

Mark learned a lot about discrimination law the hard way, didn't he? (Did we tell you that Mark skipped the part of the Company's management training that dealt with employment issues?) What if Mark had known enough about the law to seek assistance when Carl first came to him?

Suppose that Mark hadn't skipped the management training on employment issues to play a round of golf. He would have had some familiarity with the Americans With Disabilities Act, and he would have known that conditions such as Carl's may be "disabilities" under that Act. He also would have known that, if a condition might be a disability, the employer may have to determine that there is not some reasonable accommodation that might allow that person to perform satisfactorily before terminating that person because the medical condition is preventing them from performing the job as expected.

When Carl came to Mark and suggested that enlisting some help from a clerk on the mailings and getting him a printer that used different ink would allow him to perform as expected, Mark would have known that looking into those requests before responding was the prudent thing to do. At the very least, he might have consulted with the Company's human resource professionals for advice as to how to deal with the issue. In this case, he might have found that one of the clerks did, in fact, have time to assist Carl. He might have determined that one of the other printers in the office, or at least one that was readily available within the company or by relatively inexpensive purchase, used a different ink. If he had done those things, and Carl had, in fact, met expectations, then think of the tens of thousands of dollars and hundreds of hours that would have been saved.

On the other hand, even if it were determined that it was impossible to agree to Carl's requests, or if the requests had been met and Carl still didn't meet expectations, at the very least Carl's charge and the resulting lawsuit would have been more defensible and probably could have been resolved earlier and for far less money.

"Hours Wise – Months Foolish"

Across town from Mark Maverick, Emilia Heedless is focused on beating her budget for the third year in a row and getting the big bonus that would go with that accomplishment. Her branch office is flooded with business, and she hires a new administrative assistant, Marsha Meek. Marsha is an attractive young woman, fresh out of college and newly married. She settles into her new position and does an excellent job.

Emilia's assistant branch manager, Steve Hunk, is buried in work, but not buried enough that he doesn't take a special interest in Marsha. Emilia begins to notice this and is gratified that Steve is interested enough to help Marsha learn her way around the branch's business. That's the explanation Steve gives when Emilia mentions to him that he seems to be spending a lot of time around Marsha.

Two months later, Marsha comes to Emilia in tears. She recounts to Emilia that Steve has been "hitting on her" since she first arrived. She says that Steve has invited her out to dinner on two or three different occasions, has taken to rubbing her shoulders when he comes into her cubicle to ask her about something, and even patted her on the bottom once while she was bent over to get a file from a lower file cabinet. She tells Emilia that she has asked Steve to stop several times, but Steve insists that he's just trying to be friendly and continues with what he's been doing. Emilia succeeds in calming Marsha down, assures her that she will speak to Steve, and walks Marsha back to her desk.

Unfortunately, the next three weeks are very hectic, the conversation with Marsha slips Emilia's mind, and she never has the conversation with Steve. In fact, she doesn't think about the incident again until four weeks later, when Marsha calls in to say that she's not coming to work, that she's so emotionally distraught that she's seeing a psychologist, and that she can never work there again.

Two weeks later comes the charge filed with the State discrimination agency, alleging that Marsha has been the victim of sexual harassment and that, despite her complaint to the branch manager (Emilia), the company took no action to stop the harassment, and it ultimately became so severe as to make Marsha's continued employment untenable and "constructively" discharged her.

Marsha's settlement demands are so high that the company decides to take its chances and go to court with the claim.

It turns out that according to Marsha, in the three weeks after she had complained to Emilia, Steve had increased his activities. He began to insist that she go out with him and threatened her with loss of her job and that he would spread rumors that she was sleeping with him, if she did not meet his sexual demands. Again, according to Marsha, on several occasions, Steve began to fondle her at times when there was no one else around in the office. According to her psychologist, she was so emotionally distraught that she had been unable to return to work and might not be able to return to work anywhere for some years. On top of everything else, her young marriage had broken up. Despite some evidence that the marriage had been in trouble from the start, Marsha testified that her marriage had broken up as a result of rumors that she was having an affair with Steve, rumors which she attributed to Steve.

After weeks of preparation and seven days of trial, during which Emilia got very little done other than work related to the trial, the jury returned a verdict for Marsha. As a result, Marsha was awarded $40,000.00 in back pay, $200,000.00 in front pay, $150,000.00 in compensation for emotional harm, and another $150,000.00 in punitive damages for a total of $540,000.00. In addition, the court awarded attorney fees, which amounted to another $150,000.00, and costs, including expert fees, of $20,000.00. All of this was charged by the company to Emilia's branch. Needless to say, she didn't beat her budget that year. Nor did she see a penny of a bonus.

Emilia, like Mark, learned the lesson the hard way. What if Emilia had known enough about the law to seek assistance when Marsha first came to her?

Emilia, like Mark, probably would have known to contact her human resources representative to get advice. The company human resources representative would have worked with Emilia to conduct an investigation of Marsha's complaint. Whether Emilia or another person would have conducted the investigation, Steve would certainly have been questioned about whether the alleged conduct had taken place. If the evidence suggested that Marsha's complaint was true, a decision would have been made as to the appropriate discipline for Steve's conduct. At the very least, he would have been warned to cease that conduct. If it turned out that his conduct was serious enough to warrant, he might even have been terminated. One way or the other, it is unlikely that he would have continued, let alone expanded, his harassment of Marsha. The result is that Marsha's departure and charge probably would not have happened.

What if the investigation didn't show enough evidence to conclude that Steve had actually engaged in misconduct? In that case, Steve probably would have been warned that, even though the investigation didn't support the allegations, he should always bear in mind the company's policy against sexual harassment. Marsha would have been told that the evidence was inconclusive but that she should renew her complaint if, in fact, such activity were to occur in the future. Again, if Steve had in fact engaged in misconduct, he would be less likely to continue to do so in the future, given the process that he had just been through. On the other hand, if Marsha had eventually filed a claim, Emilia and the company would probably have had a better defense based on their investigation and remedial action.

Keeping Track of the Rules

Every business is subject to laws in a multitude of areas. For many of these areas, such as laws governing real estate, insurance, licensing, and commercial transactions, the corporate office will be responsible for taking most of the steps necessary for compliance and will provide the forms and instructions for the branch to follow in order to comply. As long as the branch follows those instructions, there is little opportunity for the branch to make a serious misstep. Because there is such a wide variety in the types of businesses operating through branches, it is beyond the scope of this book to try and delineate every specific law with which a branch manager is likely to have to cope.

It is possible in particular industries to pick out some of the laws for which a branch manager is likely going to have to play a significant compliance role. For example, if you are the manager of a restaurant, you, as store manager, are almost certainly going to play a role in ensuring compliance with state and local health and safety codes, particularly in those involving food handling and cleanliness of food preparation areas. If you happen to be the branch manager for a stock brokerage, you certainly are going to play some role in ensuring compliance with the various federal and state laws governing securities transactions and reporting.

One set of laws generally covering every branch office are those governing employment. If there is even one employee other than the branch manager in the branch, the branch manager is going to have to deal with employment issues from time to time. Obviously, the more employees, the more chances there are for the branch manager to experience employment laws first hand. These laws govern a wide variety of issues. Moreover, perhaps as much as in any area of legal regulation, employment carries with it the potential for significant rewards and significant penalties.

The reward of focusing on good employment practices is found in the quality of the branch work force. Attention to hiring the right people with the right qualifications for the jobs in the branch will inevitably lead to greater productivity and contribute to a better financial outcome in the branch. As is demonstrated in the examples that we have given, failure to pay attention to employment issues leads to an unhappy and less productive work force and, where attention is not paid to potential legal issues, litigation and significant costs to the business. The benefits to a branch manager of understanding at least enough about employment law to understand when a situation might entail some risks that warrant your getting assistance cannot be overstated.

Employment laws that a branch manager might reasonably expect to have to deal with at one time or another include those governing:

- The use of child labor.
- Minimum wages and overtime pay.
  - Did you know that the fact that an employee is paid salary doesn't necessarily mean that he or she is exempt from overtime pay requirements?
  - Did you know that the determination of whether an individual is an exempt employee is based on the specific duties performed by that individual, not on title or generalized expectations?
- Leave for family and medical situations.
- Discrimination in hiring, promotion, termination, pay, and any other terms or conditions of employment on the basis of race, color, national origin, age, gender, religion, military status, disability, marital status (in some locations), sexual preference (in some locations).
- Harassment by supervisors, co-employees, and in some locations, customers, when the harassment is based on gender, age, disability, race, national origin, color, or religion.
- Affirmative action obligations for federal and in some locations, state or local government contractors.
- Work place safety and health standards.
- Immigration, including whom an employer in the United States may employ and requirements for verifying applicants' authorization to work in the United States.
- The employment of members and former members of the uniformed armed services.
- Garnishment of wages.
- Payment of prevailing wages and benefits in fulfilling certain government construction, supply, and service contracts.
- Use of polygraph tests.
- Accessing employee telephone communications and e-mail.

- Protection of confidential employee information.
- Dealing with employee rights under the National Labor Relations Act, such as the rights to form or be involved in unions, to engage in collective activity even in the absence of the union, to have a co-employee present in meetings with management in which discipline may be an outcome.
- Protection for whistle blowers.
- Retaliating by discipline, discharge, or other acts negatively impacting an employee because an employee has asserted a right protected by law or has opposed company actions that he or she contends are in violation of the law.
- The creation of contractual obligations with employees, even in the absence of a written contract.
- Torts for which liability may be found, including defamation, intentional infliction of emotional distress, negligence, negligent hiring, negligent supervision, and similar torts.
- Employee benefits.

This is not an exhaustive list of laws governing employment. It should, however, give an idea of the (1) extent of the regulation of the employment relationship and (2) how important it is for the branch or store manager to have at least a basic understanding of the activities that are regulated by law, so as to allow him or her to respond appropriately when legal challenges arise.

Environment

Site Selection & Design:
Michael A.P. Casolo, AIA, NCARB (Managing Director, Waldners NY)

Employee Selection:
Steve Mills (SVP, Management Recruiters International)
Christian Schley (Vice President, The Alexander Group)

Employee Migration:
Barb Heinzel, CRP (Relocation Expert, Century 21)

Branch Process/Technology:
Emilio Umeoka (President & Director General, Microsoft Brazil)

Site Selection & Design

A field office is more than four walls. It's more than a door with a keyhole. It's more than square footage. A field office is usually your local center for creating and maintaining customer intimacy. USI's experience and research reveals that proper site selection and real estate management can reduce costs, while quickly and dramatically improving local customer intimacy.

As you seek to put inventory and decision-making closer to your customers, where are the right places to do that – and what should those sites look like?

Almost every business benefits when it increases customer traffic through its field locations. What is the first impression your offices make on visiting customers?

This chapter was written in collaboration with
Michael A. P. Casolo, AIA, NCARB.

Mr. Casolo is the Managing Director of Waldners NY, a Steelcase dealership in Manhattan. Formerly, he served as the President of USI Design & Construction Services, Inc and Senior Partner of United Systems Integrators Corporation ("USI"). Through his work with USI, Mr. Casolo has helped major national corporations with a total of over 25,000 remote site locations to plan, design, build out and manage their real estate footprint. Both Waldners NY and USI have extensive experience in industries such as financial services, staffing services and manufacturing sales & service operations.

Mr. Casolo serves as a founding member of the Branch Productivity Institute's BPI Congress.

Most highly successful business models seek field input, but do not perpetually rely on highly individualized, constantly evolving criteria for site selection and design. Instead there is agreement on a real estate platform that merely needs to be replicated (not reinvented!) in each target market. Who owns the decision-making and planning responsibility relative to real estate in your company's business model?

How will the use of this space make us money? Why this local investment – what will the space be used for? How can the space (location, design, image, etc.) help support the broader business goals?

Can proper real estate management be a value-add for your organization? Is that value-add more likely if the real estate program is centralized or perpetually left to local decision-making?

"Who's Got Time for Real Estate Planning…We've Got to Open Some Offices!"

CorGoInc ("CGI") is a rapidly growing[14] consulting firm – it specializes in improving corporate governance within Fortune 1000 companies. Having recently sought and secured funding for expansion, CGI decides to open 50 remote site locations within the next 12 months.

The company has a culture of "empowerment" so it delegates all site selection and design to its newly hired or promoted local managers – after all, "These are the men and women who have made CGI what it is today!" A deadline is set. By the time it arrives, we have a snapshot of how things are going. Of the 50 branches the company hoped to open, only 35 are ready for business on deadline.

Of the 35 open today, there is no consistent look and half are over budget on expenses – leases and buildouts were negotiated locally with the help of residential realtors who were friends of the local CGI manager. Of those 35 that are open, sixteen are in locations which are convenient to the manager (near their houses and country clubs) but to no one else. Four are in buildings actually owned by the local CGI manager, where he now gets to double-dip as landlord. Two commissioned by "Primadonna Paul" have fireplaces, showers and employee "rec rooms" tiled in Italian limestone; 75 miles away "Cheapskate Charlie" has renovated an abandoned crack-house and the loft over an asbestos reclamation facility.

Hmm…is there really such a thing as "the right deal on the wrong space?" No, there isn't. Here are some very common examples of "right deal on the wrong space…"

• The branch managers that open offices to be convenient to their house.

- The branch managers that use the realtor who sold them their house.
- The branch manager that is also a real estate investor and owns the building.
- The branch manager that has a dramatically different concept of "image" for the office and location than the corporation does (either up or down - either a Primadonna or a Pennypincher).
- Not considering the client or end user of the space (i.e., accessibility, parking, etc.).
- Not considering what role flexibility of expansion/contraction plays in the decision.
- Not considering the layout and configuration of the space in relation to how the business needs to operate (not all spaces are created equal...).
- Not considering "total cost" including build-out, FFE and signage, etc. (i.e., one space may have higher rent per SF, but may lay out more efficiently therefore requiring less space, for a total net savings).

Establishing a corporate standard with field input would have saved CGI a lot of money and headaches. Engaging a professional, objective negotiator could have trimmed 20% or more off the costs of the project. Negotiation is more than puffing out the chest and bargaining for a low cost per square foot – that's about 10% of the value created in real estate expansion. USI's research indicates that the things that happen <u>before</u> and <u>after</u> the negotiation are even more important than the deal itself – and that's what we will uncover in this chapter.

From a corporate perspective, there are basically three events which drive significant change in a company's real estate portfolio.

1. Consolidation & Space Reduction
2. Office Opening Campaigns
3. Campaigns to Maximize Space Efficiency

All three of these initiatives can be executed with greater speed and accuracy when informed by a proven strategy and process.

The View from the Local Market

Real estate is more than a line item on the financial statements. It's also the place your employees go to work every day. It's the place your customers imagine when they think about your brand. So let's spend a few moments considering the very important local perspective.

Interviews with local branch personnel and their customers revealed that their expectations from a real estate perspective are fairly straightforward.

- Cost Effective – no one wants to be stuck with an oversized monthly payment.
- Easy Access to Customers – the site's proximity to customers reduces wasted travel time.
- Right Size – not a lot of dead space, but not overly cramped either.
- Right Configuration – where the layout does not inhibit the activities necessary for success. For example, in an organization where constant collaboration is necessary, it could be a mistake to select a configuration consisting exclusively of private offices and little public space.
- Clean and Well-Kept – having visited offices in over 25 states, it's amazing how disheveled some are in their appearance. Adequate storage is a major component of this expectation.
- Safe – security for the building is adequate.
- Properly wired to support company's technology tools.

Do you see anything on that short list that could not be accomplished through a centralized process? No. So why is real estate acquisition so often left to the local market participants, whose time would be better spent on sales, marketing and service issues? Where the local markets insist on local involvement, it is usually because they do not trust the result they will get from their corporate support team. Fix the trust issue first and the local markets will gladly embrace support for corporate real estate support. Why? Because they'd rather be selling!

Worst, Best & Emerging Practices

Historically Prominent Mistakes in Real Estate Asset Management

- Relying solely on local preference (or a part-time corporate administrator) to execute real estate decisions, which has historically resulted in overpayments of 10 – 15%, on top of branding and inefficiency problems.
- Juggling a collection of internally created, or externally furnished, Excel spreadsheets.
- Overpayments on CAM charges ("Common Area Maintenance").
- Failure to take advantage of tenant improvement funds.
- Missing renewal options, which can have economic or business interruption implications, or both.
- Signing leases before planning ahead; this results in leases that are too long or too short, too large or too small.
- Allowing too many deviations from the brand standard, and creating a corporate culture where there is the belief that "the squeaky wheel gets the grease."
- Ignoring or underutilizing the leverage you have as a multiple branch organization.
- Being pennywise and pound foolish: making decisions which have

lower initial costs but significantly higher operational or life-cycle costs.

- Setting up corporate policies and practices that enable bad behavior (e.g., a staffing company that, when an office was closed and relocated because Branch & Line Management thought that a different location would be more successful, did not charge the Branch P&L for the old rent prior to sublet. This left the company with a lot of sublease space on its books, with no direct accountability.)

Best Practices in Real Estate Management

- Setting real estate direction collaboratively, but making day-to-day decisions through a focused, empowered, contact point.
- Utilizing industry benchmark data, including where competitors are opening (and closing) offices.
- Understanding Your Portfolio: having a good, strong, accurate lease database (including location, correspondence contact, terms of lease, options).
- Proactive Management: subleasing unused space, negotiating early exit options, flexible options for different modes (growth, contraction, status quo).
- Exploring creative financing opportunities (such as synthetic leases, credit sale/leasebacks); what are the treasury functions?
- Refining or Defining the company's Real Estate Strategy.
- Increasing CFO involvement in the real estate process.
- Getting excess real estate off the balance sheet.
- Putting branches inside your customers' key operations.
- Using each local space to reinforce branding.
- Bringing franchisees and licensees into the fold through a comprehensive support strategy.
- Periodically benchmarking your deployment of real estate assets.
- Using a well-defined process, the USI Eight-Step Real Estate Process is shown below as an example.

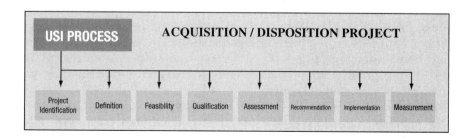

USI PROCESS — ACQUISITION / DISPOSITION PROJECT

Project Identification | Definition | Feasibility | Qualification | Assessment | Recommendation | Implementation | Measurement

Best Practices in Workplace Design

- Considering upfront costs vs. life-cycle costs in selecting materials, finishes and technology solutions.
- Designing a space which supports your company image and goals (the "face to the customer").
- Designing "bottom up" versus "top down" – not automatically accepting preconceived norms but rather looking at what your company needs to be successful.
- Considering the role technology will play today and going-forward within the space and what affect it should have on the design and build-out.
- Considering the importance of flexibility in the space – should access flooring, demountable partitions/moveable walls, wireless networking etc. be utilized in order to maximize flexibility and reduce future reconfiguration costs?
- Thinking about how "green" a company you want (or need) to be – designing to Leeds certification levels, specifying renewable or recycled materials, etc.

Emerging Practices

- Rethinking the definition of space in a technology enabled world.
- Rooting out inefficiencies/corruption as part of a corporate governance program and reinvesting the savings in revenue-producing areas.
- Improved accuracy in measuring return on real estate assets including having the right systems in place to gather, track and analyze the data.
- Tying real estate management to other core initiatives (e.g., increasing customer count, reducing employee turnover, increasing Innovation). Did you know that in most branch-driven businesses, Real Estate spend is right up there in top corporate spends with HR and Technology ("The Big Three")? Real estate management, therefore, should be close to the heart of the C-suite. Most organizations don't have the data and/or the technology to enable this relationship.
- Using real estate as a reward – recognizing top performance by giving "design upgrades" can align the company's goals with a tangible, lasting reminder.
- Real estate direction affects HR, IT, Marketing and Core Business – overall policies, procedures and goals should be set with input from all stakeholders, but to get the work executed efficiently, there needs to be one go-to decision-maker who is charged with balancing the needs of all the stakeholders.
- **Seeing the Forest & The Trees** - an individual branch tells a story, but many organizations stop listening after each branch's story is told. Progressive organizations are discovering new ways to use the collective data on their branches and are building their real estate

management processes around repeating successes (and avoiding future failures).

Questions for the Home Office

What are the primary functions of the corporate/home office? Signature image? Operational functionality? Branding?

Are those functions currently served by the corporate office's current location and design?

Has a purchase vs. lease analysis been done?

What are the current tax, privacy and cost-considerations of relocation to a more business-friendly state?

When considering the corporate location – and current plans for field expansion or contraction, are you interested in learning more about where your competitors are opening and closing offices? Demographic data on openings and closings is available through www.branchproductivity.com. This trend information can be used to great advantage in forecasting and negotiation.

Professional Real Estate Asset Management – What is the Cost?

By investing 2-3% of the real estate portfolio expense in a professional management system, it is not uncommon to realize savings of 10-15% over the life of the engagement. Thus every $1.00 wisely spent in this area returns approximately $5.00 in savings and efficiency.

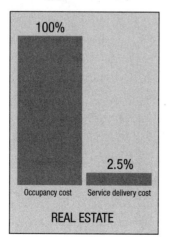

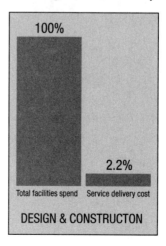

This is one of the few areas in corporate asset management where greater results can be achieved at the same time expenses are reduced.

Employee Selection

Employee selection means hiring and retaining qualified staff. If the most significant spend in a field operation is personnel, what's the best way to spend that money? What can we learn from the practices developed by the companies that hire the most field personnel?

The starting point is to recognize the type of person that thrives in a field, as opposed to corporate, environment. What kind of person thrives in a field operating environment? How do we attract and retain more of that kind of person to our businesses?

To get the answers to these questions, we turn to a gentleman whose firm is involved in more branch, store and field management positions than any other direct recruiting company. We also spoke with an executive recruiter who gave us a perspective on recruiting in the world of professional services firms and not-for-profits with geographically distributed presences.

This chapter was written in cooperation with
Steve Mills and Christian Schley.

Mr. Mills is the SVP for MRI, a global management recruiting firm whose specialties including recruiting branch, store and mid-level management. An Englishman, Mr. Mills managed 250 offices outside the U.S. as SVP of MRI Worldwide before taking his current position supporting the company's entire network (including U.S. operations). So far this year, they have trained 1300 people face-to-face on recruiting practices.

Ms. Schley is a VP for The Alexander Group, an executive search firm, where she specializes in recruiting attorneys and executives for professional services firms and not-for-profit organizations. She is an attorney who left private practice to serve in a business development capacity.

When your core business is recruiting middle management in the $75k to $150k salary band, or attorneys making $200k to $500k and up, there is a strategy to finding these people and capturing their interest.

That strategy often revolves around serving the market challengers (those in the #3 to #20 position in their industry) and helping them build a more competitive workforce. These companies and firms don't have a fuzzy concept of what "competitive workforce" means. They know it means a workforce that is creating market share and profitability.

The funny thing about hiring is it's just a means to an end. Hiring is always about change. It may be that a leader's role is that of a sales manager and sales are not being met. It may be that employee turnover under a given manager is causing problems in quality and brand integrity. But no company or firm starts with the premise of "we want to hire someone just because..." There's always an underlying business reason and it's compelling enough to require a change.

During an economic cycle where margins are being squeezed, the change desired is a return to health. During a boom cycle, the change desired is to capture market share as it is accelerating. The number one request seen in the demographics we serve is someone who can drive sales. And since the best salespeople don't always make the best sales managers, that has created an opportunity for outside employee selection on two fronts: (1) the company does not want to recruit someone from the existing sales force to manage his or her former peers, and (2) a prior placement of a top salesperson in the sales manager role may not be working so the company seeks a remedy.

Another frequent request in branch or store based operations is the Regional Manager. What you tend to find is that the move from Branch Manager to Regional Manager is one of toughest moves. That person goes from instant hands-on contact with his local operation to settling for more limited time with each direct report. He or she can't call a team meeting on 30 seconds notice. There's less reliance placed on instant decision-making and more on Discipline and structure, systems in place that repeat regularly and support a standard across the network.

To excel at recruiting field management, you have to see the positions as more than a title and a compensation plan. You need to understand what the company is trying to accomplish and why.

For example, you have to know that an effective Regional Manager will understand which metrics drive the business and keep the conversation focused on those issues. They're reliable communicators

– and now over the phone instead of in-person since they can only be in one place at once, that's another big difference from being a lower level manager.

The other challenge in regional management is some people think that it's a corporate job: it's not! It is a field-based job. It's moving people, running a region from a region, not from an ivory tower. It's true that there are many of the same questions you thought about as a Branch Manager, but now you're dealing with different Environments at different performance levels. An additional challenge for the new Regional Manager is that it may have been a while since that RM worked with underperformers; after all you don't get promoted by having a bad branch or area. A good question in an interview is to ask what type of checklists the person is accustomed to using: ultimately the good ones want a system in place that can almost run without them.

You know how you never see a seagull standing still, it seems like they are always moving. Effective field managers get their Branch Managers to act as if they are always there. They do that by targeting action-based metrics, like sales and budget requirements.

Retail management differs from office management in the respect that it is often less sales-oriented and more about the store's look and feel, the Environment. The retail manager typically needs to understand merchandising, marketing and human resources on a deeper level than the office manager.

Recruiting for Professional Services Firms (law, accounting, engineering, consulting firms) differs from retail in obvious ways. There's no inventory management involved and no street traffic to manage. Recruiting for Professional Services Firms can easily be contrasted with other types of office-based businesses as well. Sales ability is respected, but given the genteel moniker of "rainmaking." Academic credentials continue to carry weight well into a person's professional career. And many professionals resist the branch label, instead preferring to be seen as part of a global organization whose local office just happens to be located here ("don't call it a branch!").

There is increased interest within professional sectors for people who can run a business, not just practice law, for example. Hence the competition for qualified Chief Operating Officers, Chief Marketing Officers, and Chief Financial Officers who understand the nuances of professional services. What used to be called an Executive Director now is the COO: this reflects a shift toward more corporate thinking on the part of these firms.

The Hiring Process

To start with, let's recognize that for every regional manager there are 30 branch managers, so there ought to be some pretty clear criteria related to the fit you seek. Otherwise, you will be crushed by the range of applicants. Not by the choice available to you, but by the distraction of unqualified people.

From the recruiter's standpoint, the hiring process starts with a job opening and a clear timeline of what needs to happen at each stage. The experienced applicant will expect to receive a clear job description, which sounds obvious, but is often overlooked in the race to schedule an interview.

The job description should contain roles, accountabilities and measures. The biggest failing in many job descriptions today is that they are very wooly. They are written with a bunch of fuzzy objectives. This makes not only hiring, but also management, of the person more difficult. It makes it easier to hire the person you like instead of the skill set you need, which is obviously dangerous.

This example of a solid approach to field hiring was developed by MRI based on their experience with tens of thousands of interviews:

Resume Review

Phone Screen

Preparing for the First Interview

Assessment and Testing

Structured Interview, with pre-planned questions

"Day in the Field" and Second Interviews

Roles, Accountabilities and Measures (RAM) discussion

Make offer verbally, rather than by letter or e-mail

Reference & Background Checks

Written Offer

By sharing this process with the applicant at the beginning, he or she understands there is a process involved and that it will take a predictable amount of time. Without knowing this upfront, an applicant may enter into a selection process, get frustrated with its pace and unpredictability, and drop out thinking, "They are just stringing me along."

Selecting the right person also involves asking the right types of questions. Above, we refer to behavioral interviewing. This is an approach that asks for examples of a person's qualities, as well as for disconfirming evidence. For example, instead of listening to an applicant talk about their loyalty or work ethic, you might ask, "Tell me about a time where you had to commit personal time to a work project." And then the follow-up, "Tell me about a time where you had to prioritize a personal issue over a work responsibility." A telling question that comes from left field and gets around the anticipated, "What are your weaknesses?" question is "What will you be most glad to leave behind you at your current job?" This will usually provoke an honest and quick response... and it gives you the real reason they are leaving or what they really are not good at or hate doing.

The kind of applicants you want to hire for field positions are a balance of an entrepreneur and an organizational type. They respect rules (won't run the brand into the ground locally), but aren't the type to wait, wait, wait for permission to do something. They are action-oriented, within reasonable boundaries. The right candidate will come prepared to the interview and will certainly have prepared for some of your "tough questions."

Here are some questions the company should be prepared to answer:

1. Why is this position open?
2. The person who used to hold this position, how long were they in it?
3. Where are they now (are they working for a competitor)?
4. What are you trying to accomplish by filling this position?
5. What are the reasons why a person should say "no" to this job offer?
6. Is this field operation profitable? If not, why not? (Note: Human Resources and the field management often have a very different understanding of why a particular profit center is struggling.)
7. Is the company profitable (in the case of a private company)?
8. What does the compensation plan look like for this position's direct reports?
9. What is the employee turnover rate among the direct reports for this position?
10. Can you describe the career path for my people here?

What about things that really hurt the hiring process? And won't we see that many of them were avoidable through better planning and execution in the hiring process?

#1 is **desperation**! Even the most seasoned executives have been know to hire the best of the worst, instead of waiting for the best candidate.

This is followed by **disconnect**, where the individual coming in expects one thing, and the company expects another. The problems start coming in on the first day. This happens when there is less than full disclosure about financial condition or job responsibilities.

Next is **culture shock**. A person recruited from a market leader may be surprised to see that there are fewer resources available than at the former employer.

Using a recruiter that **doesn't really understand** the requirements of the position or the industry. This could be someone inside or outside the organization. The best external recruiters have moved away from a transactional sale and focus more on a relationship sale where they know as much about the needs of the hiring manager as the hiring manager does.

Limiting your choices to **people you know**. The higher level the position, the more this becomes problematic under corporate governance standards as well.

Limiting your choices to people who respond to **advertisements** (on-line or otherwise). If we go back to the original premise, that the purpose of hiring is not just to fill a position, but also to solve a business problem (one worth millions of dollars at the management level), why not actively hunt for that person?

Once the Person is Hired

Earlier (in Chapter 10) was one newly hired RVP's 100-Day Plan for making a difference in her new company. But what about from the company's perspective? What can the employer do to improve performance of the new hire?

The biggest complaint heard from new hires that quit early has to do with the hiring process: "They didn't tell the truth." Assuming you've told the truth, the next best thing to do is get them involved with feedback early and often. Regular conference calls and meetings, sharing best practices, even just unloading. It's an occupational hazard for field management that it can be a pretty lonely job: even if you have a local staff, no one local has the same responsibilities of that field manager – that's the nature of working in the field!

Review the simple, most important elements of Brand Discipline: what activities are measured and why. How to address current gaps.

Review the simple, most important elements of Environment: what an office is supposed to look like. How people are hired and developed. How the systems work. What the policies are and why they matter.

Employee selection is all about attracting and retaining individuals who can work with a team to solve problems and create opportunities. In the end, your company's DNA is made up of the people who choose to work there and the habits they bring along for the ride. The <u>company's</u> hiring habits send a message about how Discipline is regarded within its Environment.

Employee Migration

Employee migration from branch-to-branch works only to the extent that it addresses *Discipline, Environment and Innovation...*

You've got a market that's under-performing. A measured look at the competitive landscape suggests that local economics are not the reason. You decide it's time for a change.

Interviews with local applicants are promising, but then you remember something. So were the first (and second and third) rounds of interviews when you hired locals earlier!

Further reflection reveals that there is a shrinking window of opportunity and you cannot afford to mis-hire again. You want to replicate the success you've had in a similar market, so your search leads you away from external candidates and toward a proven performer located in a different market.

> *This chapter was written in cooperation with Barbara Heinzel, CRP (Certified Relocation Professional).*
>
> *Ms. Heinzel is a relocation expert within the Century 21 organization. She has served as a board member for the non profit organization Inrelco, which is dedicated to understanding and improving the relocation process.*
>
> *During the past 17 years, she has met countless relocating executives and spouses and heard, in confidence, their concerns and objectives. From those drive-time conversations, and her personal involvement in successful migration, she shares the experience of the "corporate immigrant."*
>
> *Ms. Heinzel serves as a founding member of the Branch Productivity Institute's BPI Congress.*

That's where the relocation process begins: sometimes the best way to enhance field performance is to take a proven resource and relocate that resource to a branch or store with issues the person has experience addressing. This usually occurs when the importance of changing a given location's performance significantly outweighs the resources available locally at that time in the market.

This chapter discusses how to reduce the risk in employee relocation – from the standpoint of both the company and the employee!

Goals of Relocation

It's all about speed. It's kind of like a Napa Valley vineyard deciding to use seeds from France. Given a hundred years to work with, the local vineyard might eventually produce the perfect grape. But it decides it doesn't want to wait a hundred years. The climate's right, the processes make sense, but importation appears to have better prospects than breeding!

There are many types of environmental factors that lead a company to consider relocation. They include:

- Structural events such as Mergers/Acquisitions/Downsizing
- Corporate Culture prefers existing employees
- Company resources are not matched to existing geographical opportunities
- A tight hiring market
- The existing employee is a better investment than a new hire
- Non-compete Agreement presents challenges in the local market for an attractive candidate

All these reasons make relocation seem like a natural event, but in fact it is extremely unnatural: the fact is that the average American moves within 8 miles of his or her current dwelling. So a relocation to another city or state may seem logical from a corporate asset perspective, but it is out of the ordinary for the average worker.

Why and when do employees choose relocation?

This has changed dramatically over the years. In the past, there was a great deal more reciprocal employer/employee loyalty. The letters IBM used to stand for "I've Been Moved" to a lot of IBM career professionals who moved from one branch to another for reasons of promotion or simply for project assignment.

And benefits based on tenure were much richer in the past, which encouraged employees to take one for the team.

Now, many employees view relocation as something they have to do to keep their job. At the same time, that job has fewer guarantees.

To use a historical example, where employees used to relocate to be part of the Gold Rush, now they often do so to escape the Potato Famine. These are often professionals in their late 30s to mid 40s who are facing the intersection of pending college costs for their kids at the same time that their career prospects with new companies are growing cloudier.

So the relocation is viewed as a way to preserve a current lifestyle rather than the yellow brick road of days past. See the difference from the company and individual perspectives? For the company, it's about speed. For the individual, it's opportunity or fear of loss.

Costs of Relocation

What should a company pay for in terms of transferring one employee?

There are many variables but a few averages come into play:

- ~ 30 – 40% of the transferred employee's salary, or
- ~ 20% of the transferred employee's home value (the one he or she sells), or
- ~ $55,000.

Obviously there are huge differences in relocation costs, mostly based on the wage scale of employee being transferred. Little of the variation today comes from the negotiation skills of the employee or the human resources department; most companies have fairly well-defined parameters under which they make the economic commitment to the move.

There are three places to reduce the expense for the company without putting the burden squarely on the employee's shoulders. Those come in areas of negotiated agreements with movers, realtors and temporary housing providers.

Some of the typical elements that are considered (and possibly awarded) in a relocation package include, on the Buy Side:

- Two house hunting trips to the new market (for the employee and the spouse, if applicable), two to three days each.
- Location Tour &/or Facility Tour, especially for the spouse.
- Moving expenses. Assigning these directly to the company, rather than reimbursing the employee for out-of-pocket expense, may result in more favorable tax treatment for both parties. Many companies agree on a cap in this area.

- Closing costs, including mortgage points required to match the interest rate on the previously owned home. For example, if an employee had a 6% interest rate and is being moved in an interest rate environment where he or she has to now pay 7.5%, the company may consider buying down the interest rate to reflect the current cost of money.
- Temporary housing. This is less common as many employees want to move just once. A three-month maximum is common.
- Goods storage.
- Shipping the cars.
- Spousal assistance for employment. This may have peaked in the 1990s.
- Sandwich generation assistance. This is where the employee has dependent children and parents that require relocation. A fairly unusual benefit today.
- Gross-ups. This is a catch-all where taxable income to the employee is grossed up to cover any resulting tax obligations. For example, an employee in a 30% tax bracket who receives $20,000 in phantom income through the relo may also receive $8,571 to cover his or her tax obligation ($28,571 in income would require a $8,751 tax payment in a 30% tax bracket).

There is another aspect to consider on the <u>Sale Side</u>, where there are generally just two expense factors:

- Closing Costs
- Real Estate Commissions, which may be negotiated

In the past, companies would sometimes allow the employee to bypass the hassle of selling by literally buying the employee's original residence and writing the employee a check so they could quickly move on to the relocation.

Today there is a growing resistance to taking the employee's house into inventory, where the employee merrily goes on their way without having to sell the original domicile. This is typically found only in very large corporations and at the senior executive level.

The way this works, when used, may look like this:

1. Pre-marketing assistance is offered, where the employee is given an incentive to sell the original home on their own.
2. After a 60-90 day window, the opportunity to sell on one's own expires. At this point, a Third Party or the corporation itself buys the original home based on appraisals.

There also may be a variation of this process, which is known as an amended sale. This is where an in-house program assists with pre-marketing. Once there's an offer, the homeowner may negotiate the offer, but does not sign a home purchase contract. The homeowner agrees on price, terms, inspection issues if any (and is responsible for rectifying out-of-pocket expenses), but does not sign off on the contract. Instead, the homeowner issues a quitclaim deed to a Third Party so that the Third Party is the owner of record until the transaction is closed. The homeowner gets a check from the Third Party for net proceeds prior to closing.

Dangers of Relocation

When a relo goes bad, it doesn't usually happen quietly. It blows up on you. What are the major issues related to relocation that can torpedo the company's goals of speed to market and the employee's goals of security and/or opportunity?

The biggest wild card in the equation is often the spouse, and they are sometimes resistant, despite the friendly face they put on publicly during the experience. It should be expected that there will be concerns about the purchase of a new home, nostalgia for local relationships that will evaporate, changes in educational opportunities for the children, cost-of-living differences, and even security concerns. A friend of ours relocated from Houston to a large commercial center in South America. The two children had to start attending private schools and were driven to school by an armed bodyguard. That's more than an expense to consider.

Let's consider this upheaval from the employees' family's perspective:

• Change in direct management. Will we get along with the new boss(es)?
• Cost-of-Living Sticker Shock. When people are asked to relocate from Indiana to Chicago, they can't believe it: "I've got a pond, I've got acres, now I have to live on a postage-stamp lot and I can hardly afford that!" And moving from anywhere to California is a rude awakening.
• Children's Activity. "My kid has a great relationship with her gymnastics coach. I don't know if she will want to start over with someone else."
• Education. The standards vary greatly from state-to-state and district-to-district.
• Neighborhood. Is the employee moving from a suburban to an urban environment...or vice versa?
• Sheer Mileage...I'll be far from family and friends, the things that really matter!

These are the issues that The Boss doesn't hear about from the suck-it-up employee, but you can be sure the employee discusses with his or her spouse daily during the relo process. One experienced realtor shared this common quote from people on their first House Hunting Trip: "I'm going to be transferred...I'm not sure if I'm going to accept the job."

Often, the momentum for or against the relo decision is based on the first House Hunting visit, which is a sobering thought when you consider this is a $55,000 average business expense.

Lifespan of the Relocation

How long does it take for the corporate asset (the relocating employee) to be repositioned in the new market?

The single greatest factor in determining speed to new market is the sale of the original home and purchase of the new home, attended by the move of the family. These lynchpin factors drive not only the physical relocation, but the emotional recommitment as well: finding the house makes the employee and spouse feel better.

Where this process differs from a typical move (under eight miles) is that the relo has to move at warp speed. Where it may be OK for the eight-miler to take six to nine months preparing the old house for sale and shopping around, most relo transactions take place within 90 days: once the new market commitment is established, both the employee and the employer are eager to move things along.

Paradoxically, the longer the distance, the faster the transaction needs to be. Kind of like ripping off the band-aid!

Migrating Technical Skills vs. Management Skills

Which is more likely to move apace – and stick: the technical migration or the manager migration? There doesn't appear to be a lot of data on this question. Anecdotal evidence from realtors involved in these transactions shows a few differences in the way a scientist might approach the relo vs. the method used by a sales manager.

Technical employees tend to be more analytical, do more research, and take longer to make up their minds. Contrast this with the P&L Manager, who knows that all this upheaval equates to downtime for productivity: the P&L Manager may instantly feel like a lame duck in his or her original position and be anxious about making timely changes to the new facility. Increased time may lead to diminished outcome.

For the P&L Manager in particular, speed is of the essence. Get it done, get them up and running, get them in their new positions, and take away their uncertainty (which minimizes stress). There is a real tension here because most people want to take more time on bigger decisions. One solution is the introduction of an experienced, objective third party, whose motto should be: better, calmer, faster!

Relocation is not a decision. It is a series of decisions...

Go/No-Go Threshold	Party Asking
Can the Needy Market can be well-served by employee from the place called "Somewhere Else"?	Company
Internal or External Relo?	Company
Have we found the right person, thus validating initial relo decision?	Company
Can we establish Terms of Offer that make economic sense for both parties?	Company
Would I even consider relo?	Employee
Will the effect on my family be positive, or at least neutral?	Employee
I would only consider if...	Employee
What will happen if I say no?	Employee
How does life here compare with life there?	Employee
Formally accept offer?	Employee
Following the formal acceptance, how is this whole moving thing going – is it too much hassle?	Employee
Now that the move is over, is this working?	Employee
Now that the move is over, is this working?	Company

Thirteen go/no-go thresholds to be negotiated! That's a lot of times to be right, isn't it? What if the first decision (about not needing an employee with local market knowledge) was wrong? The silver lining in all this: when it works, the loyalty of the company to the employee and vice versa can be strengthened measurably.

What makes the migration worth its attendant risk is the successful dissemination of knowledge and experience to markets where it would have taken far too long to grow it locally. Like the Napa vineyard where the grapes survived the journey and now have taken root: you've built something locally that wouldn't be there without the relo.

When you hear the inquiry, "<u>I don't care where they are</u>: who can get this done for us?" Follow up with the question, "How will this employee migration specifically affect the target operation's Discipline, Environment and Innovation?"

Branch Process/Technology

Assuming a 36 month depreciation schedule for technology assets – and current expensing of non-depreciable items, the typical company today may spend $5,000 – 6,000 per year per employee on these types of tools. How do you maximize that return on investment? We'll start by looking beyond the tools and focusing on the tasks to which they are applied...

Is it harder to sell and manage today?

Yes. And no. On both counts...

Despite human nature and the timeless belief that today's challenges are greater than yesterday's, if you step back and think about the resources available to a businessperson today, there are many advantages today.

If you ask your salespeople if it is easier or harder to sell and manage today than it was just a few years ago, the vast majority will answer, "Harder." Yet if you consider the elements within the process by which most field operations go to market, those elements are often more

---

This chapter was written in cooperation with Emilio Umeoka.

Mr. Umeoka is the President & Director General of Microsoft Brazil. He started his career as a petroleum engineer in Angola, and later founded an independent software development company before working with Compaq, where he was responsible for their Latin American Commercial PC Business. At Microsoft, he manages internal operations and customer relationships in the Brazilian market. In this chapter, he and Frank discuss the ways that a technology driven company uses technology itself to drive sales and operations.

Mr. Umeoka serves as a founding member of the Branch Productivity Institute's BPI Congress.

---

controllable than they were even ten years ago. One of the major opportunities for executives managing field operations today is the use of technology to save time and better manage customer information.

Element	More resources available?	Or fewer options?
Meetings with branches	X	
Access to information	X	
Time management	X	
Access to clients	X	

So the real answer to the question, "Is it harder to sell and manage today?" is that the bar has been raised, but there are better tools available to help you clear that bar. It doesn't feel easier, and maybe it isn't. But there are vastly more tools available today to the manager of field operations than there were even five years ago.

Let's move away from theory and talk practically. Most field offices are dedicated to sales and customer service, so we'll use examples from those areas.

We conduct meetings electronically and at Microsoft there are two types I'd like to share with you. The first is when I am discussing operations with my peers from 70 different countries. So there are 70 country managers on the phone, the speaker talks via this conference call on a PC and we can all see his or her materials using Office Live Meeting and PowerPoint during that presentation.

Does this completely replace the in-person meetings among peers? Of course not. But think about the efficiencies gained by holding that meeting via PCs instead of the alternatives: if everyone had to fly to headquarters, it would cost significantly more and we would not communicate as often. And the online distribution of information via PowerPoint means that the speaker has the flexibility to adapt the presentation up to the last minute. In fact, even beyond the last minute - we ask questions online during the presentation and they are addressed immediately when that is possible.

The second type of electronic meeting is more local or regional in nature. For these we use VTC, Visual Teleconferencing, for larger branches, or webcasting generally. Again, this is not a complete substitute for face time. But it allows management to reduce travel time and travel expense. More importantly, it addresses every salesforce's need for mobility and flexibility. We take advantage of the wireless network so people can participate in meetings no matter where they are. And the webcasts are recorded so that customer appointments never need to be rescheduled – the salesperson can view the content at a time that does not interfere with sales activity.

Resource	Usage	Considerations
Live Meeting (e.g., Office Live Meeting)	Web conferencing Internal Meetings Customer Meetings	Reliability Security Ease-of-Use Flexibility Playback Options
Mobile Devices (e.g., Pocket PC, Smartphone)	CRM Enterprise Resource Planning	Personal Info Mgmt Documents E-mail, Web browser Photo recording Infrared Beaming Instant Messaging
Collaborative Websites (e.g., SharePoint)	Share information Collaborate on documents Collect team knowledge	Security User flexibility
Single Message Box (eg., Avaya Unified Messenger")	One collection/ distribution point for voice mail, e-mail and fax messages.	Security Ease of integration

Improving Communication

When you step back from the technology and think about what you are trying to accomplish in business, it often boils down to communication.

What generates esprit de corps or its unwanted alternative, poor morale? Strengths or weaknesses in communication. The ability to get feedback. The ability to record, access, analyze and address internal issues.

What improves customer relations? Being prepared. Understanding changes in the customer's business. Being accessible.

Anyone can see how the proper application of information technology is an asset is these areas. Access is much easier and quicker today. We can more easily share challenges and success stories, and have more ways to ask for feedback. Even the personal, face-to-face, meeting has the potential to be more meaningful today – it is easier to prepare for and it says, "I care enough to be here in person."

So much information related to vendors, customers and partners is now available, that every step in the sales process can be performed with more skill and knowledge. Think about it: historic purchases, usage trends, information on major competitors, boards of directors and executive bios. All this used to be "in the head" of each rep if they were doing they job well, which increased the risk exposure if this rep decided to leave with all this information and no records stayed within the company. Now it is much easier to access and that results in greater intellectual liquidity within organizations.

We see great improvements coming in several areas. Voice-over IP, which gives the user flexibility and savings. Wi-Fi hotspots. The convergence of telecom, entertainment and IT. Think about the ways you can improve your customer's experience by getting creative in these areas.

We have a golden rule: the more face-time with customers, the better. Now, the customer is probably wrestling with greater responsibilities and fewer resources (who isn't?). So the customer does not have the luxury of spending time with a salesperson or technical support person just for the sake of spending time. They expect value from each and every meeting. This is not a competitive secret – companies that seek to avoid commoditization are moving more and more to the high-end. They are thinking about how they provide value-added Innovation for their customers.

Interestingly, Innovation is probably going to be one of the two biggest brakes on outsourcing (the other is regulation). The #1 question for a company seeking cost-efficiencies through outsourcing (especially offshore outsourcing) is not, "How much can I save today?" The #1 question is, "How much labor am I willing to transfer without transferring my intellectual property?" The answer to this question is tied directly to the idea of improving the customer experience. Face time is one thing you cannot outsource to an offshore resource!

Challenges in Successfully Automating the Sales/Service Process

1. Time

CRM is a five-year commitment. Most sales vice-presidents in America, as an example, have an average tenure half that length at best. The tension there is obvious.

The sales team is accountable for results this quarter. Sales leadership seeks to change customer action <u>this quarter</u>. CRM changes the way the sales force behaves over <u>years</u>, so it requires a great deal of strategic commitment.

2. Change

A significant commitment to change management, and alignment of processes, is necessary to achieve maximum return on technology investments. If you've been listening to your sales force, you already know the biggest behavioral change – getting people to recognize the value of data input and retrieval.

We wrote earlier about the risk inherent in any process where the individual sales rep decides which information stays in his or her head. Few salespeople welcome additional record-keeping – or any change to their process for that matter – so their needs in this area must be addressed not ignored. On balance, the company's need for consistency in customer relations usually outweighs the individual salesperson's need for convenience. Any change management in this area must recognize that CRM is not a substitute for curbside coaching and that the recording of activity never trumps the activity itself: activity and recording must co-exist, not be presented as a choice.

3. Reality

CRM amplifies the amount of mistakes if you have poor processes to begin with. Now this is a real opportunity as well. It forces the sales leadership to consider questions like

❑ What really is our sales process here?
❑ What do we really need to know about our customers and prospects?
❑ How can we better track cross-selling and referral opportunities?
❑ What communication between sales and service is required?
❑ How do we satisfy management's need for information depth,
   without turning our sales force into data entry operators?

Technology Strategies for the Nimble Company

Microsoft in Brazil is a small- to mid-sized company. We have the benefit of the brand's standards, but try to operate with the flexibility of a smaller organization. And I ran a small software development company for nine years, so I am familiar with the challenges our smaller customers face in their markets.

The initial advice I would give to an executive in a small- to mid-sized company is, "Take advantage of your greatest natural strength: speed and agility in the decision-making process." Putting decision-making closer to your customers, through field offices, is critically important.

Secondly, keep it simple. There are many companies using Microsoft CRM integrated with Outlook. Remember when you used to have to refer to a series of codes whenever you wanted to save, print or edit data? System training could take the better part of a week. Now, people are able to be up and running within an hour. Keep it simple and people will not only be productive faster, but they will be more consistent in their use of the tools.

Third, utilize cross-reporting and cross-sponsorship. Sales and operations/service sit together during meetings. Plus we use an Ambassador concept in my group: subject matter experts travel from different locations and support other field offices, sponsoring initiatives in their "adopted" offices.

Work/Life Balance

Effective field managers constantly ask themselves and their people, "What are the best ways to create synergy between the main office and the branches?"

This starts with the goal of making each branch feel like part of the whole company. One way to do this is by addressing universal goals like "work/life balance." After all, everyone seeks this to some degree.

Microsoft Brazil has implemented some programs that take place simultaneously, like a Family Day for the offices which all happen at the same time. We also have Citizenship Programs to uniformly recognize contributions from different areas.

This matters in the context of technology because, at the end of the day, technology is supposed to make business easier and more efficient. And if you can achieve synchronization with positive events, it lays the groundwork for consistency in the harder business processes as well.

Innovation

The Field of Vision – Replicating Best Branch Practices:
Genia Spencer (Managing Director, Operations, Randstad North America)

Branch Intelligence:
Brett Norgaard (Chief Research Officer, Wire the Market)

New Product Impact Testing:
Beth Kulick (Senior Consultant, Automation Associates)

Balancing Innovation with Compliance
Ted Long (VP National Programs, Comsys)

The Field of Vision - Replicating Best Branch Practices

What is a best practice?

It's a job well done! It's an activity that increases sales, improves quality or improves the brand: the elements identified earlier as the three goals common to all field operations. Which best practices are worth replicating?

• The ones that your customers care about. If a best practice creates the opportunity for greater sales and/or greater margin, it matters.

• The ones that are scaleable. If an activity is positive, but not scaleable, it may be worth attention on a local level – but doesn't have the profit potential required in a national or global campaign. That doesn't mean forget about it: everything is scaleable at a certain price point. If your clients would pay more for something new done consistently,

This chapter was written in cooperation with Genia Spencer. Ms. Spencer is the Managing Director of Operations for Randstad North America.

She has directed the operations of over 400 domestic field locations, focusing on improvements in the area of sales, quality and brand management. Her experience spans B2B and retail.

Ms. Spencer serves as a founding member of the Branch Productivity Institute's BPI Congress.

they have the opportunity to make it scaleable through the price point.

• The ones that may be unique to your brand. If a best practice can help you advance your brand, it matters. It's important to realize in this category that a brand cannot last indefinitely without increased sales and/or a continuing quality advantage, so resist promoting the brand with best practices that don't address sales or quality as a ingredient.

How do we find the best practices worth replicating? And, just as importantly, how do we avoid the distraction of picking the wrong ones to institutionalize?

Start by limiting – not your search – but the number of best practices on which you plan to focus your commitment. Research shows that you can only coherently present three major differentiators without diluting your message. Differentiation is kind of like a wedding toast. One or two, maybe three, highlights can make a point beautifully. But who remembers the particulars of the bloviator who has ten different nice things to say? We get it, already! And by the way, we lost your one good point somewhere. Stop while you're ahead.

Where do you find the highlights?

<u>Ask your customers.</u> If you don't do this, you run the risk of "talking to the mirror." It may feel good to self-analyze, to contemplate one's navel, but that exercise won't make a difference in the things that matter. You need to let your customers' interests drive this type of initiative – and you do that by giving them a peek inside the windows of your branches.

A common trap here is to ask, "What do you like best about our relationship today?" Or, "What would you like to change about your current relationship?" These are fine questions, but the answers you get won't really provide answers to these questions. People say what they think you want to hear. The far better approach is to use a behavioral method that captures the motivation behind actual events. For example, "Tell me about the last time you switched suppliers."

You can learn more about the relationship between the government and the governed by examining an actual revolution (why they attacked and killed their leaders) than you can by polling people and asking them, "What do you like best about your government today?"

Once you've got a list of best practices to start with, then pick three that you are absolutely passionate about. At Randstad these are called "*Strong Concepts.*" These universally effective levers should form the basis of your business model. Once that model has been identified, it should be preserved in the corporate culture through execution and recognition. If the model constantly changes, it is weakened and its dilution is assured, so find a model that allows sufficient flex on a local basis.

The importance of a model increases with the number of markets it attempts to serve. There is no point in being a global brand without customers being able to count on a certain "Wow" factor from every location.

Let's be honest. Field modeling cannot be abdicated to what feels good in each of your 500 (or 5000) locations at the moment. And Monday morning e-mail may be interesting, but it does not compel changes in behavior. Field locations want strategic direction that quickly translates into competitive advantage – and that's not an ad hoc process. It requires market sensitivity and executive sponsorship. The fuel: clarity, passion, communication and reinforcement.

The cornerstone of modeling is that business owners need to own it. It starts at the very top of the organization. Relying solely on the goodwill and enthusiasm of people left without direction is a recipe for brand inconsistency. Management, the operational leadership, needs to own the teaching of the concept. Contrast this with the approach favored by many bureaucracies where the Training Department owns the concept. No, for true replication, best practices need to be owned by management and spread throughout the field organization.

What does ownership mean? Well, it's more than the rollout! The reality today is that auditing matters. When you inspect what you expect, you get two things: improved compliance and a stronger quality template to prove excellence in the marketplace. This inspection is strengthened when it contains an element of independence. Independence in two ways. First, the metrics are objective enough that compliance is evident on its face. Second, some level of Third Party review is integrated to reduce bias and ensure objectivity.

Pitfalls in Replicating Best Practices

Why doesn't passion for a new idea always win the day? Because process matters, too. The dangers underlying the replication of best practices are potent. And the first danger reflects the greatest strength and weakness of operating via the field model. **The first danger is overcomplication**. A complicated message has the potential to be misunderstood exponentially with the number of locations to which it is addressed. Each of your field locations probably has an existing practice that may be in conflict with the improvement sought, so the one cancels the other out. General Electric is a leader in using workout sessions to decide what needs to be taken away to ensure impact. This approach goes beyond saying, "We have a good idea." It recognizes that something may need to moved out to make way for the next initiative. This approach not only protects against piling on, but also sends a message that the corporation is so committed to the new idea that it is willing to sacrifice something for it.

The second danger is not knowing what good looks like. Field personnel generally recognize what constitutes true differentiation and what's going to end up in the trash dump as last month's "Flavor of the Month." But this natural intuition will be corroded in the organization that constantly peppers its field with worthless initiatives. To avoid not knowing what good looks like, go to top-performing offices. And by the way, you don't have to limit your observation to your own offices. What about your customers' top locations? Your competitors? Consider other businesses with a reputation for sales growth, quality and brand strength.

When we say, "Go to top-performing offices!" – we don't mean stop at the door. The <u>customers'</u> <u>perceptions</u> of those offices can be as meaningful as what actually goes on within the four walls. Go to the top-performing offices of other companies through an organization like the Branch Productivity Institute (www.branchproductivity.com). Benchmark client and employee impressions and what matters to them. But take the next step as well: ask the same questions consistently of the <u>lower</u> performing offices. This is a step many companies don't take.

It's natural for someone to react, "If I want to understand Beethoven, and I've got season tickets to the Chicago Symphony Orchestra, why do I also need to hear the junior high school band play his work?" It's a fair question. Here's the hard answer: if you were leading the CSO, you wouldn't need to. But you're not leading the CSO in every field operation. You've got some locations playing at the junior high level and they need you to understand the difference between their practice and that of the professionals.

The third danger is that not everyone understands that they need help. One leading industry association recently reported to its members that customers scored the members at 65% on the three things that mattered most. That 65% is barely a "D" but I'll bet the companies represented therein didn't rate their people a "D" average on their recent performance reviews, in their shiny Annual Reports, in their back-slapping visits by regional managers. So who's right? The customers? The self-grading employers? Capitalism means the money gets to grade the performance – and the people with the money are the customers. This is all just one way of saying that not everyone feels they need the help; or if they do, they won't automatically believe that this corporate program is the help they need.

A final note on dangers in the context of acquisition: avoid pandering. Pandering to acquisitions, keeping people happy, offering "pretend involvement" in exchange for some level of "welcome to the family acceptance." A corporate culture requires leadership – it is not a melting pot. Why do so many acquisitions fail? One reason is the temptation to pour everything that made the acquired company successful into the acquiring company's culture: the outcome is like mixing together 31 flavors of ice cream, there's nothing strong about it. What once was distinctive is now muddy.

Yes, respect what is great from new contributors. But be clear about your own model for growth. Hopefully you don't acquire if they don't meet that model in the first place. And if a part of the acquisition is not going to fit, don't force it. Spin it off or shut it down. Don't keep one group hanging out there that operates in conflict with the rest.

Finding the Message That Will Change Behavior

Let's say you're aware of the three dangers listed above. Your best practice passes the simplicity test, it clearly shows what good looks like, and your people recognize the importance of improvement. Pause for a moment and congratulate your team: many corporate initiatives die for failing to reach your current progress point.

What's next? How do progressive organizations conduct the alchemy converting message into behavior?

Genia has developed a Bowtie Methodology that maps out participation in the process, so the message doesn't stay just a message:

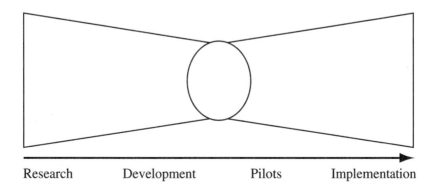

Research   Development   Pilots   Implementation

At the beginning, on the left, you want to represent the needs and concerns of as many people as possible. This can be done through statistical sampling, but the idea is to include the energy and input of as many interested parties as possible. This will include employees responsible for execution, customers, and prospects. It may also include investors, suppliers, channel partners, and others as well.

The basic idea: cast a wide net. And ask questions that reflect behavior. If your initiative seeks to improve customer and employee loyalty, ask why they have historically changed jobs or suppliers. If you seek to improve quality or reduce costs, ask why a guarantee was necessary. Let the parties questioned know that the organization is committed to making a change in a certain, already-defined area, and it needs their help in targeting its resources. Also ask the party questioned how they would like to be involved in the rollout of any solution.

Moving to the right on the bowtie, some part of the population will have no interest in participating, so the size of the group narrows with their non-involvement. Your Marketing Strategy Organization will work with the smaller group to confirm respondent needs and wants. Once this takes place, you are reaching the center of the bowtie. At the core, establish a team of people with cross-functional experience:

- Sales & Marketing, to measure market differentiation potential.
- Financial analysis, to assess costs and return.
- IT, for automation.
- Customers, for sanity check.
- Field operations staff, to consider (like GE) integration with existing practices and whether any need to be sacrificed.
- Organizational Development/Training, to gauge whether there is a method by which this change could be rapidly trained.
- HR, to link to performance management and rewards programs.
- Executive Sponsor, to coordinate and approve resources. More than an administrator to the process, the Executive Sponsor owns the ultimate success of the initiative.
- Regional Management, to be the local face of ownership.

This team establishes a timeframe for rollout, method for training, measurements and accountability. At this point, we move further to the right on the Bowtie. The selection of early adopters in a Pilot Program is critical to proving the concept so that it sells on workability ("This really works!"), not just on authority ("I said do it!").

Next after the pilot is the full roll-out and ultimately, the full execution of the new method by all locations and acceptance by the market. That's the far right side of the Bowtie, where we have come back to maximum participation.

Done the right way, the Bowtie can ensure the acceptance of your core initiatives. It may even take you to places you didn't expect to go. DuPont is in the chemical business. But it is also a model for safety. It's now to the point where DuPont not only sells chemicals, but their safety and risk management program as well. How did it get there? It listened to its people and made systematic improvements based on that input.

Unexpected Benefits

Investing in a replication process leads to more than the change itself. There is a huge connection to <u>reducing employee turnover</u>. After all, the more predictable we make someone's success, the more likely they will hold on during tough times.

The process also makes it easier to actually <u>record what was invented here</u> and integrate those ideas in the company's Branch University (introduced in Chapter Eleven). All true best practices focus on some element of Discipline, Environment or Innovation. Any time you integrate a best practice, there's a lot of history that needs to be addressed:

• Where did the need come from?
• What common language is wrapped around the initiative?
• What common history do we share?
• What are the background reasons as to why we are committed to this?

At Randstad, we like to cover this history in our on-line preparatory resources. Depending on the topic, we may combine operating owners with outside facilitators to do the in-person training. We reinforce with comprehension and skills practice eight weeks after the in-person course was delivered. This is done on-line and determines how "sticky" the training was.

The Importance of the People You Choose

The word disciple was dissected earlier to reveal its root: scienter (meaning knowledge), which is also the root of science. Who are your disciples for change?

Let's start out by recognizing that not everyone wants to be a disciple for your next initiative. We all are trying to juggle increasing workloads and many of us are on overload. To cut through the fog of over-commitment, we have to nail two things: (1) we have to reach into the passion of the person we seek to attract, and (2) our idea has to be good! If it isn't the passion will quickly be replaced with another layer of healthy skepticism.

One great thing about self-preservation, the human instinct to survive, is that it makes people naturally as resistant to bad ideas as they are to a disease. Unfortunately, some people expand this resistance to good ideas as well. How do we use this natural resistance to weed out the truly bad ideas (we all have them!) and to promote the good? Pretend you are trying to select a jury. You want to find **people who are open-minded** enough to consider and embrace alternatives. You don't want to rely 100% on true-believers from the outset. Their agenda will end up controlling the direction of your initiative, and their agenda may not be right even though it will be among those most forcefully articulated.

We can start by considering our unique audience. **Utilize the strengths, and understand the limitations, of your field operators**. For the company that chooses to operate in the field, local accessibility is key to its success. Otherwise, all their work would be done out of a call center in India. In this model, we tend to have employees who themselves use a local market approach and sales process – emphasizing community knowledge and personal relationships. They are more experienced in consultative sales than in enterprise sales. This population will bring expertise related to how things affect customers and local employees. This same population will rely on corporate expertise related to enterprise applicability. The manager in Omaha will not instinctively know what to recommend for the manager in New York City. If the Omaha manager thinks otherwise, here's a reality check. Ask Omaha, "How would you like me to rely solely on the input of New York in making decisions about the Omaha operation?" That's about the time that the clarion call of the local manager issues forth, "But he doesn't understand my market – it's different here!"

New employees can be great ambassadors – they can honestly say, "I was attracted to this new model." They have no baggage or ego/ownership around the old model. Because of that, they tend to be highly supportive of it during the implementation phase.

Customers should be chosen carefully. It is surprising how many have to get permission from their company to participate in a supplier's internal campaign. It can also be surprising how wary some of them are about sharing what you need to be world-class! They may not freely tell you. To be candid, they may not care enough about your success yet to make that contribution. The key with customer involvement is developing a process which minimizes their time investment. And just as with acquisitions, their involvement cannot look like pandering.

Try to communicate what is in it for the customer. The answer may be improved delivery of your product or service. It may be reduced usage of your type of product or service, which leads to lower expense on the part of the customer. That can still be a win if it improves customer loyalty and attracts other customers through testimonial evidence.

Corporate staff should be chosen for their systems knowledge and ability to relate to the field. There should be strong evidence of teamwork, not just individual contribution.

For the **Development Team**, find "Possibilitarians." They are the kind of people who see potential.

For **Pilot Teams**, you want high-potential employees, highly respected Influencers. You don't pilot in places that are failing; you go to places with a strong history of execution.

The **Implementation Team** should be comprised of coaches, teachers, and enablers. You want people who measure their success by how many people they've touched that are successful.

In all cases, whether you are talking about driving enterprise change or succeeding in the field, you want people with an internal locus of control. That means they believe they control most of the factors for their success. Avoid externalizers who overly blame or credit outside influences. You want high degrees of flexibility in the field, especially since the whole point of a branch is to adapt to the local market.

One staffing veteran tells the story of a recruiting trip he took in college. He visited a corporate headquarters and, surrounded by cubicles, said to himself, "I will never be one of many." He made a mental note, "These people work in cubicles." Lots of people love the Dilbert-world, but you can't be one of those people if you are in the high visibility of a branch. In a branch, nothing is predictable. This squarely contradicts with the corporate world, which tends to feel more controlled.

How Do You Measure Success?

Measurement is a lot easier if you "know what good looks like" from the get-go. But even when it is easy, it's never automatic. If a company rolls out a new replication initiative without changing its measurement system, it's fooling itself. That's like putting lipstick on the mirror.

The usual challenge, however, is not too little measurement but faulty targeting of that measurement. And faulty measurement is a chafing thing. Many industries, which for decades were built on relationships, are now so driven by Vendor Management Systems and technology that the good things behind the original customer relationships are being buried under data.

The key to balanced measurement is the regional leadership. The regional manager has to own the picture of the best practice, and has to be the most articulate person in the company regarding its importance and execution. The regional manager can't wholly abdicate the training to the Training Department. If they are going to measure, they have to be able to teach what they are measuring.

Regional Directors in Genia's world have to be more than sportscasters – people who merely report (with strong opinions!) what is going on in the league. The RDs also have to be more than just another player on the field. The RDs, whether they originally came from the field or from corporate, have to become the coaches that own the respective Win/Loss columns for their markets.

One final note on best practices, this one coming from an experienced RD: don't over-regulate. The field is more than just footprint. Its inherent strength is its local decision-making. Don't waste the resources of a branch using it primarily for enterprise sales or enterprise delivery. If more than 25% of your business in any local operation comes from national accounts, that's an opportunity to ask, "Why aren't we more a part of this local community?" Fix that challenge and you've got more than clones, you have the sources of your <u>future best practices</u>.

Branch Intelligence

Brett is contributing to the chapter on branch intelligence because he is in the intelligence business. This chapter will give a brief overview of the intelligence-gathering process, then move onto specific issues related to using your field operations as market sensors.

In his company's experience, there is much to learn from competitors and clients. Most of it hidden in a place that they are not yet willing to share with you. Because the information is hidden, we think we know more than we do. We know just enough to explain our current level of success, not to predict with accuracy why our top client is preparing to leave – or what needs our top competitor anticipates.

The reason the top 5% in a sales organization might rely on Brett's team for executive appointment-setting or insights not publicly available is simple: if you are average, you probably can't do much with a well of competitive knowledge. But the top-performer knows that's where next year's book of business is coming from.

This chapter was written in cooperation with Brett Norgaard. Mr. Norgaard is the Chief Research Officer for Wire the Market, Inc., a company he founded to serve the competitive intelligence needs of the top 5% of sales and marketing executives.

His team uncovers hidden needs and offers executive-level appointment-setting based on the nexus of their research with their clients' unique value propositions. He never bores the client, because his mission is to know something about the client's business that will surprise them.

Mr. Norgaard serves as a founding member of the Branch Productivity Institute's BPI Congress.

Brett's interest in field operations springs from the fact that any company operating under this model has a built-in network for tracking and hunting new opportunities. Sadly, few use it to its capacity. The reason visionary companies Innovate faster and more effectively is they are using their branches and stores as market sensors, not just footprint.

How do you "wire your market" to predispose your best potential clients to buying from you?

It starts by understanding your own company history and how to use that history to reduce skepticism. It continues with an understanding of the market's needs. Now, most salespeople will tell you they prepare for a sales call by visiting the prospective customer's website. That was great five years ago, but it's "me too" today. What about the stuff you won't find on the website? Can you map out their value chain? Who are their customers, their channel partners, investors and suppliers? Is their focus on new accounts, pricing strategy, bundling, exceeding service capacity? What questions do you want answered – and who has the answers to those questions? How would you find those things out about your own company?

Intelligence is not about the quick-hit. It can shorten the sales cycle, but it also enables the salesforce to hold something back, to run long-distance instead of treating every customer interaction as a sprint to the customer's wallet.

Ethically, there is a right way and a wrong way for field operations to gather competitive data. Some of the wrong ways include unethical practices such as dumpster-diving, or forming fictitious companies to gather information. Other wrong ways are not unethical, just inept. They include overkill, poor targeting, purchasing secondary sources of dubious quality. But that's the wrong way. Let's talk about the right way.

The right way starts with the premise that the customer is on our side. The customer's expectation of the salesperson's business acumen is rising because vendors no longer compete on the greasy handshake and the trip to Happy Hour. Competitive intelligence fits into the broader category of business acumen: it's the surprise. It's said, "There is no learning without surprise" and without new information, the sales call quickly devolves into relationship-building on a personal, rather than professional level. The customer expects us to know more and more, to surprise them with new ideas; so the customer is actually on our side.

An intelligent branch builds its Discipline around only those actions that the customer values. It creates an Environment that anticipates what the customer would prefer. It structures and promotes Innovation that addresses future needs, not past losses.

Gathering Intelligence: The Process

Defense

First, do no harm…an intelligent branch protects and defends its own information through the use of proprietary systems, management involvement and employment agreements. This defense occurs throughout, but is not limited to, the gathering, analysis, dissemination and action phases.

Gathering

An intelligent branch gathers information from the right people. If you were a Republican pollster and you wanted to know what support your candidate had in the local market, you wouldn't interview only Republicans! But that's what field operatives do when they limit their discussion of customer needs to current customers, or to those prospects that are unhappy enough with their current supplier to meet with a new suitor. What about the people who won't meet with you? Isn't finding out what they want even more important? But that's the challenge in relying solely on the salesforce for data gathering.

Can we turn the salesforce into field-based intelligence operatives? It's very hard for several reasons. One, their highest use is generating revenue not information. Two, as anyone who has gone through a CRM initiative can attest, they hate recording information consistently. Three, many salespeople we've talked to do not want to take something upstairs to Marketing and see them get the credit: they'd rather use the information to local advantage.

Don't give up on the salesforce as your front line in this effort, however. It can be done. It starts with Marketing providing value to the salesperson (whose primary focus is to sell more stuff). It evolves to the point where the salesperson thinks, "if I bring these marketing nuggets back, I make more money." For it to work, you can't have field operatives or corporate staff being judgmental or conservative. Maybe you leave the information on a 1-800 line…and there's no penalty if a rumor proves to be false. By the way, branches are excellent rumor validators: they live by the grapevine and if 30 of your 200 locations report the same rumor, it helps for a central source at corporate to see that.

Another sorting mechanism is facts vs. conclusions. One possible review of a sales representative's trip to a trade show to gather information:"It was great." What does that mean? He had fun? We don't need a performance evaluation from the rep. Instead, we want facts. Who was there from this list? Which of our customers did you see visiting with competitors? Why? Is Brand X making delivery commitments on their new product yet? When? The place for conclusions is in the analysis, not the gathering.

Analysis

One early sorting mechanism that will speed the analysis of the data gathered is to train gatherers to collect both Explicit Knowledge (the customer opened a new distribution center last quarter) and Tacit Knowledge (why).

In analysis, an intelligent field operation looks beyond the obvious, but it doesn't ignore the obvious! Local market analysis, by its nature, provides weak conclusions of national perspective, because the branch is mostly interested in its local issues (duh!). If you doubt that, ask a branch why they don't want to whole-heartedly embrace the analysis of a branch manager elsewhere: "My market's different!"

This phase of the operation also benefits from a dedicated perspective. Just as a corporate marketing type can't go in the field and instantly match the sales activity of a top salesperson, the top salesperson is probably not used to reading demographics and running comparison models. If he or she is familiar with those activities, he or she is not spending enough time selling!

A little knowledge is a dangerous thing. You may know that the company you are calling on is a market leader. But do you know that market leaders don't want to hear about best practices, they already believe they own them? After all, others copy them, not vice versa. Analysis is valuable when it suggests what to do with the knowledge, not just gives you a weather report. This is the place for conclusions, and those conclusions should always answer the question: "So what?"

Dissemination

In dissemination, like analysis, there is a role for the corporate office. Get the information out, but more importantly, help people visualize what it means. When salespeople start getting meaningful information from marketing, they begin to trust marketing and they start to give information back.

There is such a thing as too much dissemination. Too much information usually is accompanied by too little meaningful analysis. It's like the manager that sends an e-mail with 20 attachments…and the subject line is FYI. Who cares? Search engines are cheap and hard drives are big: that's why there's a lot of crap sitting out there not making anyone any money. It's why salespeople think they are uniquely prepared by visiting the website. It's why customers think they don't need a sales call because they know your prices and your products – if that's all you've got to offer, they're right, they don't need to meet you. There's no surprise, is there?

Action

This is where the branch is king. There are certain things that just jump out at a local person – and when they do, you go with your gut. But without input, there ain't gonna be no output. So the decision at some corporate centers has been to restrict distribution of data to markets that agree to participate in the data collection phase.

So the branch is king…but they've got to earn that title by giving a little something on the front end (or at least agreeing to give on the current campaign).

Using Your Market Sensors

The Big Brands spend millions of dollars figuring out what motivates consumers to either buy the Big Brand's product or abandon a competitor's. The advantage held by any company with multiple field offices is that it has a ready-made set of market sensors, from which it can perform that same market research function. But those sensors need to heighten their awareness to be truly effective – otherwise it's like asking a person without a sense of smell to be a wine-taster. Not fair to the judge. Not fair to the wine being judged.

The best place to start honing market senses is not by spying on your competitors, but by understanding your own company's history and market position. Know yourself first.

Living Without the Five Senses

Are all your field operations actively observing what is going on around them? Or are some of them walking around like zombies, never noticing the opportunities and dangers presented in their respective Environments?

Imagine your field operations as individual people.

Some have an excellent sense of smell – observing, in the course of any given day, the smell of good home cooking (receivables being converted into cash), the smell of smoke (danger in the form of poor account retention), a ripening flower (an opportunity for customer development).

Some have excellent hearing – they hear the watch-like precision in which orders are taken and filled, or the grinding of gears when things are not running smoothly.

Some have excellent vision, touch or taste – each has the potential to observe what is happening in their Environment.

Now wouldn't it be a shame if a person with great vision saw a threat before anyone else, but failed to share that observation? Or if 55 different visions of that threat were seen, but not reported? How about getting 55 reports of the threat, but none of them are in the same language? What about a blind pursuit of customers without any targeting? Those are the levels of true market feedback present in most companies today – where the field locations are not set up to feed information back to corporate in a meaningful way, and don't use all their senses to attract and retain customers on a local level either.

The field locations are precisely where competitive intelligence begins to succeed or fail. What can you do to improve or create your competitive intelligence platform? How can you create and reward Smart Branches?

What's your Branch IQ?

The traditional intelligence test is a simple formula: intellectual age divided by chronological age. The Branch IQ is just as simple: market awareness divided by chronological age.

The one-month old branch cannot be expected to know as much about their market as the 50-year old branch. But the one-month old branch must be expected to know as much about their market as every other one-month old branch.

Each company's intelligence needs, the way it defines a smart branch, are different and unique. But one example we frequently start with looks like this:

1. What is this branch's current customer count?
2. How many new customers has this branch signed up in the past three months?
3. Why did those new customers switch to our product or service?
4. Which of last year's top ten customers are down in usage?
5. Why are those former top customers using us less?
6. What is the average tenure of your employees in this branch?
7. Who are your biggest three competitors in this market?
8. How are you planning to improve customer traffic in this location over the next six months[15]?
9. Which three brand standards are most important to this branch[16]?
10. What does this branch do better than any other branch? Can you describe that strength with enough specificity that we could replicate it elsewhere[17]?

Those ten questions might represent the top part of the equation (market awareness) for you. The bottom part of the equation is simply where each branch lies on the tenure scale – so a more established branch should always be expected to have proportionally more market awareness than a startup. This exercise is easily integrated into operational reviews or office visits. It is highly effective when coupled with a quid pro quo from "the tester" – in other words, don't ask a lot of questions without also offering back some new information that will increase sales, reduce waste or more effectively promote the brand on a local level.

Where many operations stumble is when they get all their information at the startup phase and then they stop recording. There's a blitzkrieg of data-gathering at the beginning, and then the comfortable cycle of neglect sets in. Don't let that happen to you!

Wiring Your Market

When companies come to us, newly committed to wiring their market to intuitively prefer their product or service, we start by applying intelligence to the problem.

We start with a disciplined examination of the intersection of what your company does well and what the market needs. If you are investing serious money in a product launch or service campaign, you have to be willing to do more than just ask the questions. You also have to look at the landscape – what are the macro trends, why do they matter, how will they influence behavior? Who are your friends and enemies?

Friends and Enemies

- Who are the key people within your local market that can most influence your success?

- What factors are driving the decisions of those key people[18]?

- What "magic moments[19]" need to be captured and replicated within this group of advocates?

- How would you describe the <u>external</u> platform of communication you use to publicize magic moments in your business?

- How would you describe the <u>internal</u> platform of communication you use to publicize magic moments in your business?

- What co-branding opportunities exist within your local market?

- Who is working at cross purposes to your goals?

- What external factors are inhibiting growth?

- What internal factors are inhibiting growth?

- Is time a friend or an enemy to your operating style?

- Is sales call data collected and analyzed in a disciplined way? Or are we simply tracking revenue, not bothering to observe why prospects meet with us (or more importantly, why they don't meet with us – or who they are meeting with during the time slots they deny us).

You have probably noticed that competitive intelligence gathering is not just about understanding the competitors. Yes, that is a piece of the mosaic, but equally important is the knowledge related to customer motivation and your own internal history.

What do we mean by internal history? One thing that a new manager inevitably notices as he or she starts asking questions about the business is that the answer from their own employees or their corporate office is often, "I don't know." "I don't know why they stopped using us." "I don't know why they switched suppliers." "I don't know what that client's anniversary date is." Why does this knowledge gap matter? Because your internal history is the lens through which all market data is analyzed.

So who is responsible for this type of initiative? The optimistic answer is, "Everyone," and in a way that is positive, but it is also unrealistic.

While everyone should be able to participate in data collection and analysis, someone ultimately needs to be responsible for the program. There are two ways to do this effectively.

The first is to hire or select someone who owns the process. And by the process, we mean the definition, the distribution, and the reinforcement. In a branch or store setting, our firm works with a company like 3PR <u>to certify individuals</u> in this methodology. In other types of companies, we work independently.

The other alternative is to use a proven third-party resource to coordinate the field management's roll-out of the program. And then to keep the visible ownership of competitive intelligence gathering at the field management level. This tends to work best in settings where objectivity and speed are determining factors. In a branch or store setting, our firm works with a company like 3PR <u>to actually run</u> the methodology.

In either case, to avoid management by anecdote, it is best to start by planning what types of questions to ask. When this is not done, you are relying entirely on salesperson instinct and follow-up (or what questions the board intends to ask this quarter). We have a number of proprietary methods we integrate into our campaigns; here are some examples of tools we have refined with different organizations. You may already be using some of them today. The trick is aggregating them so you get a complete picture of what you need to know to win. The key to aggregation is using common tools.

Examples of Data Collection Tools

One cautionary note: just because someone owns a frying pan does not mean they are a chef. Just because a company employs salespeople to call on customers does not mean customer data is being collected in a meaningful way. The substantive content integrated into these tools is critical.

• Account Intel via Appointment Setting
• Account Intel on Appointment Rejection
• Competitor Intel
• Sales Calls
• Customer Satisfaction Surveys
• Quality Surveys
• Exit Interviews
• Trade Show Data Collection Campaigns
• Office Visits by Regional Management
• Office Visits by Corporate Staff

- Brand <u>Discipline</u> Reward Programs (see the earlier chapter by Troppe & LaPlace)
- Third Party Mystery Shopping
- Accounts Receivable Management
- Client Anniversary Lists
- Company History Calendar
- Win/Loss Analysis

Examples of Data Application

- Sales Calls
- Sales Collateral
- Breakfast Briefings on Trends Important to Customers
- Brand <u>Innovation</u> Reward Programs
- Efficiency Campaigns (see the earlier chapter on Replicating Best Practices by Troppe & Spencer)
- Establishment of Acquisition Criteria
- Establishment of Brand Standards

<u>Is it Better to Look Smart – Or to Be Smart?</u>

In applying your data, it is better <u>to be smart</u> than to look smart. Of the brands you say you most admire, how many made that list because you admire the "smarts" of the brand managers in the business. Few, if any. Instead, you admire those brands' application of their competitive intelligence rather than the actual collection and analysis itself.

This is all just a fancy way of saying you don't perform competitive intelligence just for its own sake. Companies today cannot afford to contemplate their collective navels just because smart people need jobs in marketing. Rather, those companies execute from a competitive analysis platform because it makes more customers want to purchase more of what they offer, more frequently, and at a premium price.

So, remember, we are not here to look smart. We are here to create little magnets that draw customers to our brand. If you look smart in the process, that's great, but it's not the end game. No one likes the pointy-headed expert that fails to generate revenue.

The bottom line on smart branches and field operations in general: every location that is generating revenue should also be generating data. This leads to faster, more effective product development, increased account retention rates, and shortened sales cycles. It also creates a side benefit: increased employee morale. In our experience, the more employees know about their company's history, place in the market and competitive advantage, the more likely they are to stay in the organization. Furthermore, the "field agent" who is part of the data collection and analysis reinforces their commitment to the company every time they come back to their local manager, or to corporate, with a new nugget of information.

New Product Impact Testing - From Concept Validation to Productivity Standards

Think about the last time your organization introduced a new product. Maybe you're presently in the middle of such a campaign. Maybe it's been years. Few things vary as much as different companies' commitments to new product development.

Whether it is part of your corporate charter to introduce "x" new products every year, or you embark on that new product development only sporadically, if you've been there, you know one thing for sure...

This chapter was written in cooperation with Beth Kulick.

Ms. Kulick is a Senior Consultant with Automation Associates, Inc. Automation Associates, Inc. is the leading independent simulations/solutions firm in the world. With over 500 projects completed in sectors ranging from production to distribution retailing, the firm's representative clients include Starbucks Coffee, Yum! Brands and Booz Allen.

Beth has been involved with the lifecycle of developing retail stores, from conceptualization to operational deployment. If you are an American consumer, you have experienced at least one of Automation Associates' business models.

Ms. Kulick serves as a founding member of the Branch Productivity Institute's BPI Congress.

There is only one thing that will kill a new product rollout faster than over-engineering the whole process. What is that one thing? Failing to plan at all. Successful Innovators realize the direct connection between the strength of their development process and speed to market.

Experience with new product development reveals a spectrum of approach. At one end of the spectrum is the company that over-tests. What is the cost of over-testing?

• Time
• Money
• First-mover advantage
• Market Share
• Morale

At the other end of the spectrum: the company that expects every "good idea" to be so good that momentum alone will carry the day. The dangers here…

• Diminished loyalty to the brand (when customer service expectations are not met)
• Time and money (correcting and re-correcting errors)
• Morale ("When are those guys at corporate going to give me something I can actually sell?")
• Loss of Other Good Ideas (when the process is flawed, it limits the company's ability to quickly and efficiently evaluate which ideas will really be money-makers)

It is important to note that a new idea is not always a new product. The new idea could also be the enhancement of an existing product, the fine-tuning of an existing process, or the resurrection of a dying (dead?) brand. One currently popular idea among multi-brand organizations is to consider co-branding and retrofitting stores to improve capacity utilization of existing infrastructure: it is one of the ways to increase same-store sales with minimal investment. Another advantage of co-branding as an idea: you may get a whole new demographic coming into your store.

So what are the most popular ways to use new ideas make you money?

• Increasing sales per customer.
• Shortening the sales cycle.
• Increasing customer traffic, especially during non-peak periods.
• Improving capacity utilization.
• Improving reliability (thus lowering costs).
• Enhancing the Brand.

All worthy goals and the kind of stuff that gets blood pumping through the organization. After all, what happens when you have no new ideas? Or you fail to implement the best ones?

• Commoditization. The brand becomes generic.
• Dependency on current customer applications.
• Dependency on cost-efficiencies, which by definition have limited potential: you cannot drive them to zero.
• Price pressure.
• Diminished customer loyalty.
• Loss of market share to true Innovators.

Honestly, can you think of a single profitable business which fails to effectively introduce new ideas? So…what is the best process and how does it compare to yours? It's different for every organization, but here is one example used by Automation Associates to reduce risk and improve speed to market.

1. Problem Identification (Market Need)
2. Concept Development
3. Computer Simulation/Modeling: Virtual Refinement of Concepts (get you as close to reality without actually building it yet)
4. Concept Selection – which one or two appear to have the best potential?
5. Pilot Program
6. Based on lessons learned, build model store(s).
7. Deploy model(s).
8. Targeted Rollout.
9. Review and reintroduction of Productivity Standards.

Some organizations skip number three and race straight to the build-out of a physical mockup. The disadvantage there is twofold: (1) it costs more and (2) it puts a governor on your flexibility. Did you know some restaurants will throw away $100,000 worth of food created just during test mode? And delay the opportunity to identify the service redline (where systems break down)? Both unwanted expenses can be minimized through the use of sophisticated computer simulations.

Does the simulation take the place of the mockup? No, of course not. But ignoring the technology available today to simulate labor costs and service redlines is like designing a new computer without…the use of a computer! You could if you wanted to, but why would you want to?

The ultimate question in greenfield operations (which are new from the ground up) is which design (which includes staffing choices, equipment considerations, impact on other products) can most cost-effectively service my peaks? For introduction of new ideas into existing infrastructure, the question is which sales and service platform will drive sales most consistently?

Once you've built it, or rolled it out through the existing infrastructure, the question becomes, "How do I most efficiently operate these?" Automation Associates uses Point of Sale (POS) data to measure and anticipate the right mix of products, customer traffic and service levels. And this is always a moving target: there are market variables due to seasonality, regional differences, etc.

Some companies use personnel expense as a % of sales to predict labor requirements, but it's not recommended. It's like using the Farmer's Almanac to predict this year's cotton yield. It's not very sophisticated and it's usually wrong: a company can end up hiring too many or too few people because their assumptions are crude under this approach. The problem: different products and services have different labor needs. The more volatile your product mix, the more you miss your hiring projections and end up overstaffing or understaffing, either of which contributes to higher turnover…and greater volatility!

One of the flaws of this method can be turned to great competitive advantage. By using computer simulations for your labor model, you identify opportunities for slide deployment, which is another way of saying multi-tasking or switch-hitting. Let's face facts – no one <u>knows</u> what the customer will order today, you can only <u>predict</u>. And given that environment, the worst management nightmare is when every employee has to be trained to perform every function because of errors in prediction. The right question here: what is the right mixture of multiple skill sets and how do we reduce or avoid the time and expense of overtraining or undertraining?

The answer: use a proven process for concept development. Let's take a brief look at each of the nine steps in our example.

1. Problem Identification (Market Need)

This is both an internal and external question. Or, to be more precise, it is an internal question that is answered by an external question. First the internal question: what is our need? Is it (1) increased same store sales, (2) improved quality (a/k/a reduced waste or improved utilization of capacity), or (3) brand enhancement?

Next, what market need can be addressed to help us achieve this goal? If you are a service company, are your customers buying other services that they might consider buying from you? If you sell products, could you sell more of them by changing the customer experience (encouraging them to stay for dessert, especially during non-peak periods) or by offering complementary products, or services (warranties)?

The answers to these questions do not limit what you can do with your new ideas. In fact, a great new idea intuitively answers these questions. But you should go beyond intuition and quickly establish agreement that the internal and external needs intersect in a way that will make you money.

For example, what good is addressing a market need if the market expects you to do it in a way that will not increase overall sales, enhance the brand or improve your operating efficiency? Hey the market wants free beer! Let's build microbreweries in each of our field offices and give away free beer (poisoning people in the process because we're no good at it, by the way). So the point is, you can't address a market need purely for altruistic reasons – you have to consider the impact on sales, cost and brand.

What about in the other direction?

We want increased revenue! To hell with what the market wants or needs, they just need to buy more of our stuff. Work harder, you stinking employees, and force the market to respond!!! Uh, that hasn't worked, has it? There's only one institution that can mandate revenue increases: the people that hold the power to tax. And even that can't be taken too far or you have a tax revolt on your hands.

2. Concept Development

OK, so you've got an idea about your goals and how they fit with the needs of the market. This is where the creativity of your organization is put to the test. And the best companies do this better than anyone.

This step represents the first move from the general to the specific. Specifically, how do we intend to fill this market need? What expertise do we have, or can we acquire, that can be sold as a new product or service? How can we package and define that expertise in a way that magnetically attracts customer interest and demand?

There's a format for this type of exercise. With branch-based businesses, 3PR and Automation Associates conduct *Innovation Workshops* to facilitate the creation and capture of money-making ideas. It's a real treat for your employees and customers to participate in this type of exercise. Not only are you starting down the path of discovering what products and services will define your future, but you are also improving communication and morale in the process.

3. Computer Simulation/Modeling

Why this step, which "virtually" refines the concepts, getting you close to reality without yet building it? Several reasons, foremost among them being (a) improving speed to market, (b) reducing cost, and (c) reducing risk.

What capacity do you need to service your customer? How will the introduction of something new affect what already exists? What is the link between sales and service? How many intake positions can we adequately support? What is the right balance between people, space and tools[20]? What balance between internal production and external production? Where does each location start to redline?

It's a fact that most businesses live by their peaks. Whether you are in professional services, transportation, retail, production, or anything else, you have to be able to consistently meet customer demand during key periods (and those periods are usually unique to your business or industry). Failure to do so results in decreased sales, increased waste and tarnished brand.

But engineering every operation for the peaks is very time-consuming and very expensive if those peaks remain "potential" and are not actualized. So a key question here is also, how are sales and marketing integrated into the service platform so that (1) off-peak demand is created and (2) peak periods are operated at their highest profitability?

4. Concept Selection

Which one or two concepts appear to have the best potential? Based on the simulation and modeling described above, this is the place to compare the likely outcomes and decide on a course of action. If it's a tie, then which concept appears easier or less expensive to adopt? Which will be the easier to pilot?

This stage takes place on a smaller scale every day in retail, where new products compete for space and channel sponsorship. The decision usually revolves around the consideration of revenue, demographic fit, incrementalism vs. cannibalization (does the new product represent an add-on sale or a replacement sale?).

Once a decision on concept has been made, the process moves from theory to practice, and onto the actual testing ground of a pilot program.

5. Pilot Program

This is the place to work out kinks with forgiving customers – or with a smaller sample. What does the Pilot Program do? First and foremost, it protects the brand! By limiting the customer exposure to a small, controlled environment, mistakes can be caught earlier and with less global impact.

Second, the Pilot Program suggests possible problems in execution separately from distribution. The last thing you want to find out in 5000 locations at once is that the customers are interested in a slightly altered version of your offering, before you have the opportunity to address the distribution requirements in meeting that customized interest. The Pilot Program in this case may actually help redefine the product or service in Pilot.

The Pilot Program also validates lessons learned in the computer simulation stage. As the computer simulation suggests certain courses of action (maybe related to staffing roles, equipment requirements or quality checks), these can be tested in a safe, controlled Environment. Training requirements are often refined as a result of observations in the Pilot Program.

Finally, this stage continues to build enthusiasm for the new idea without distracting all your field operations from their current business.

6. Build Model Site(s)

The model may be an existing operation or a brand new site. In either case, if the Pilot Program is the alpha test, the model site is the beta test. It's not quite ready for prime time, but there's been significant data collected and processed in an effort to wow the customer when full deployment takes place.

As the building progresses, the computer simulations are revisited to check expectations versus reality. The architects work with the operations team to identify further efficiencies.

7. Deploy Model(s)

OK, people have been hired and trained. Inventory is ready to go. It's opening day! This is where the customer experiences your new idea "outside of the laboratory" for the first time. Lessons in Discipline and Environment are put to the test.

Observers from the deployment team note potential issues and training opportunities.

8. Targeted Rollout

In the beginning, you wanted customers to chase your new idea. The Pilot Program and Model Deployment suggested you're on the right track. Based on the results of the Model Deployment, you are now getting interest from across the organization's markets. It looks like your new idea is contributing to a significant increase in same-store sales and is enhancing brand loyalty.

So everyone wants to get on board. A Targeted Rollout gives you the opportunity to make money off the new idea while testing its acceptance in more than just a few places. You may decide to pick a region based on demographics or current compliance with brand standards.

The Targeted Rollout follows a strict schedule, from promotion to training to delivery. It seeks to reduce variables in execution so that any variance in customer acceptance is due to demographic preference.

9. Review and Reintroduce Productivity Standards

Ever since the Computer Simulation in Step Three, the organization has been seeking to answer questions related to how much space and labor would be required to facilitate successful deployment of the new idea. "What's it gonna cost us to run this thing?"

These are the Productivity Standards. Following the Targeted Rollout, the standards estimated are reviewed for accuracy and opportunities for improvement. What changes in the hiring or training process will improve productivity? Is the equipment and staffing adequately addressing peak requirements? Can we move the redline without disturbing quality? How do we want the managers in these locations reviewing performance?

Summary

The more field locations, the more that doing this well matters. For every thousand sites, each $20/day loss in efficiency or customer sales represents a $6,000,000 annualized problem. A corresponding gain represents cashflow, customer good will and competitive strength. How much is your next new idea worth?

Balancing Innovation with Compliance

You want to branch out – and retain the right level of local market flexibility. You want to find your field of vision. What do your markets see? What do they see, but look past, in the race to build this quarter's revenue? The perspective from the franchisee (real or potential) is one way to cut past the corporate fog.

Whether you currently operate via the franchise model, are considering an expansion into that channel, or simply hate the concept, there are lessons to be learned from the franchise experience.

To understand the Innovation/Discipline balance from the franchise perspective, one has to first understand the franchisee and how they are different from a company employee placed into a branch.

This chapter was written in cooperation with Ted Long.

Mr. Long is a VP with COMSYS, Inc. Headquartered in Houston, COMSYS provides IT support to 70% of the Fortune 50, and 35% of the Fortune 500. Mr. Long has 18 years experience working with franchise operations, which he has found to present a unique perspective on the Innovation/Discipline balancing act.

This chapter discusses some of the reasons companies choose the franchise model, and once they've done so, what they learn about "managing" entrepreneurs.

Mr. Long is a founding member of the Branch Productivity Institute's BPI Congress.

To begin with, the construction of a Uniform Franchise Offering Circular (UFOC) requires some level of Discipline. In order to organize your methodology and award franchises, you have to be able to clearly document which local actions are expected to lead to success. No one buys a franchise so they can start from Square One. Every franchisee (the local buyer/operator) expects to receive a formula, the application of which will produce results in the local market.

Beyond the UFOC, the franchisor (the corporation awarding the franchise) cannot expect to develop successful markets unless it guides the Environment and Discipline of each new operation. The opportunity to understand Innovation's and Discipline's balance is perhaps best presented through the lens of franchise operations.

Why? Because franchisees by their nature become renegades. Which is a good way to test brand opportunities, if the franchisees don't kill you in the process! Why and when do companies opt into the franchise model, in whole or in part?

- It may cost around 1/3 of the start-up expense to open a new location, because the franchisee is putting up his or her own money for most of the local expenses. This allows the franchisor to expand distribution with less capital.
- It is a creative way to grow personnel: most of the people you will attract to your franchise model would not consider a position as a staff employee: they have reached a point in their career where they are itching for an ownership opportunity.
- It is a way to more quickly establish footprint and top-line market share.
- It is a way to develop deeper local market knowledge and relationships. While everyone claims to be great at "relationship-building", franchisees are generally much more heavily networked than their branch counterparts. As a result, they know their market 10 times better than company staff.

Understanding the Franchisee

Who is he or she? Someone with business maturity who probably left the 8 – 5 world to get away from memos and politicking. Someone who may be working in the business with his or her spouse. The franchisee looks different than the corporate staff and the "company-owned" manager. The franchisee will follow the model more closely in the beginning than your branch employees. And they'll abandon it more quickly once they achieve success. The franchisee is a person that wants to know, "what's the chances that this $100,000 I have to invest will be worth $1 million in ten years?"

Do you have occasional bouts of "us vs. them" (or a Culture Gap between corporate and the field, as described in the Periodic Table of Branch Vices)? In a franchise operation, the potential for this syndrome is even more prevalent – that's the tradeoff for all the benefits listed above. When you are dealing with real entrepreneurs, who have skin in the game, the expectation level rises a few notches. It's like working with a partner instead of an employee. If you've ever worked with a partner, you know what I mean.

Many companies stumble early on with franchises due to the simple fact that they are used to working with branches, not independent owners. This is a challenge for the branch staff, who are used to going to regional leadership to resolve account questions or disputes: that regional leadership can't just act on gut instinct when it comes to franchise rights and responsibilities. First of all, the franchisee does not work for the regional manager. Secondly, there is a written contract that both parties are obligated to follow. It takes a little of the spontaneity out of the relationship.

But it's an even bigger challenge for the corporate staff. The franchisee is much more quick to point out that, "I pay your salary!" Now the branch manager could say the same thing, but there's something about having your own money invested in the business – and being responsible for your own payroll – that makes those words come forth much quicker. Aside from the customer-expectation possessed by many franchisees, there is also a slightly different focus.

The franchisee is less likely to call corporate about an HR or IT issue, much more likely to focus on items related to cash. Remember, the franchisee is not angling for promotion or political acceptance: he or she will hone in on the accuracy of financial statements, collection activities, co-op funds, anything that has a direct cash connection.

Most people at corporate will say, "We do a good job with our reporting and servicing the field. Why are those franchisees such a headache – I'm doing the best I can!" A corporate staffer thinks they understand the financial pressures of the franchisee, but they often don't: they have to learn them.

An exercise Ted used to help address this problem (fixing it requires more than one exercise) looked like this:

He brought the corporate department heads to a conference room. He gave them each a checkbook with $100,000 in it. And then walked them through the costs of running a franchise. For the First Month, they had to make withdrawals for rent, personnel, telephone, advertising, technology, franchise allocation. And there's not a whole *lot of revenue that first month, so the deposit was much smaller than the expenses.*

Months Two – Five looked only incrementally better. And in Month Six, there's a current profit of $2,000. Yeehaw! Oh, except the kid's tuition is due. And, just as a reminder, these franchisees were paying all their living expenses out of another checkbook while the business was in start-up mode.

We're talking about people's life savings. How long would it take you, an Accounts Payable Supervisor, to save $100,000? How would you feel watching it slowly bleed away during startup? The franchisee is not using Monopoly money: he or she is handing out many years' worth of savings. And trusting that the corporate office of the franchisor is on his or her team to make this work.

It gives a little different perspective doesn't it? It doesn't mean the corporate staff should take abuse, but it gives a great framework for understanding which requests are unreasonable and which are fair. That's just the first six months: just beyond breakeven is when things start to get even more challenging.

As the franchise relationship matures, money continues to dominate the discussion – but in a different way. While the early franchisee is focused primarily on cash flow and this month's reports and this week's support, the tenured franchisee sees these items recede to a (close) second. What moves in front of this month's check? Expectations of Innovation and improved corporate support.

One reason franchisees went the route of a partnership instead of starting cold on their own was they expected <u>proven processes</u> and <u>brand strength</u>. They want to align with a front-runner and they expect to be taught. And once they've stopped learning the basics and have a profitable business, they look around and say, "What am I paying you 40% of my gross margin for?"

They expect that the novelty of the initial relationship should continue. "What have you done for me lately?" And this is the hardest part of franchising: you can't rely solely on the contract to keep the franchisee engaged. Sure, it's a legally enforceable agreement, so they're not going to run across the street and open a competing operation. But no one likes the feeling of indentured servitude: how do you continually provide value back to the franchisee?

Who determines what value is? The financial analysts at corporate? The lawyers drafting the UFOC? No, the franchisee determines value: what can you do next to help them get what they want?

Goals vary by individual. Short term, the franchisee may want a new cabin cruiser, or to give his or kids a choice where to go to school. A bigger house. The opportunity to build something that his or her child could run in five years. Longer term, it depends on the company's strategy related to renewal or buybacks.

Whatever the individual's goals, these are the things the franchisor wants to leverage in order to get the things corporate wants. If corporate wants to implement a price increase, it has to link that increase to the franchisee's personal goals, it can't just say, "Do It" and wait for the franchisee to jump on board.

Using the Franchise to Balance Discipline with Innovation

So these are the people you're working with. Let's say you've done a good job of attracting franchisees that, once they've signed up, are solely interested in the success of this franchise – they aren't juggling cash and time conflicts with other businesses. They are sales-oriented. They are compliant early and anxious soon after that. They're putting your claim that, "You want entrepreneurs and decision-makers working here" to the test!

One franchisee for a global staffing company had an operation in Erie, PA. His style rubbed a lot of people the wrong way – he once showed up for a company costume party wearing an adult diaper and smoking a cigar. Instead of shaking hands with the President when receiving an award, he kissed him. He once sponsored a "typewriter toss" at a local bar to promote his secretarial recruiting. He wasn't reserved and polite like most the corporate support people he interacted with.

Frank got to see a different side of this franchisee – when working as a Regional Franchise Consultant for this company he visited his operation on numerous occasions. The "crazy franchisee" would take corporate visitors to a fish-stick plant at 9:00 p.m. to meet the second shift supervisors. He would personally check in his workers at 6:00 a.m. at a plastic extrusion facility. He would put an injured employee to work in his office until the injury healed. His office's wall was covered with photographs of customer locations – above them, the heading, "You Can Judge Us By The Companies We Keep."

This franchisee showed off more new ideas in a two-day corporate sales visit than a person would see in a month of polite discussion at corporate. About 20% of his market probably couldn't stand him, but the other 80% loved him – and that 80% definitely included his staff.

The company ended up buying him out (for millions) and then wondered disappointedly why revenue didn't continue to grow at the same pace once he and his partner were gone.

How do you use a guy like this? What about another franchisee, a woman in Toledo, OH who built a 10,000 hour/week staffing business in about 18 months? What about a family that built an $80 million franchise in Chicago? These people owned their businesses – they lived and breathed them. Whether that business had good company-owned managers as well is beside the point: of course it did, Frank started his career as one of them. But the experience at that company was richer because of these franchisees who risked their savings and tried crazy new ideas.

The way to use these types of people:

- Understand the <u>Environment</u> in which they operate. Is their office in a different type of location? What type of people are they hiring? How are they communicating goals? How are they using the company's technology and processes to make money?
- Examine their commitment to <u>Discipline</u>. What activities do they perform with consistency? Which brand standards mean the most to them?
- Consider adopting those things they introduced into the business that fall outside the current model.
- Use them as examples of what local market knowledge and networking can accomplish – they are a potent image to company-owned branches that are struggling to define themselves.

Most importantly, tap into what's important to them:

- Name Awareness – they chose this franchise because they believed in the brand. They want to be associated with a winner; it validates their original purchase agreement.
- Their Cash Flow – are there resources you can award based on growth in performance?
- Financial Stability of the Company – a local franchisee is stronger when he or she is affiliated with a financially healthy franchisor.
- Extending the Company's History of Innovation – the franchise prospect wants to see something you've done that's unique in your industry. That curiosity doesn't die once they start working with you.
- Developing their Managers – many franchisees want to see the day where they can rely on their local manager(s) to run more and more of the business. What can you do to help their manager(s) stay out of trouble (for example, HR support) or develop in their professional careers (such as advanced training in the areas of sales, financial management, or staff development)?

If you have franchisees, ask them how they believe they can contribute to the company's ongoing history of Innovation. If you don't have franchisees, consider how the last ten memos from corporate might have been received from an audience with their own money in the business. Did they create value <u>worth paying for</u>?

If you franchise, or you don't, take a look at the way successful franchise operations in your industry are selling their concept. Remember, these people (by law) have to document their unique service concept in a UFOC. We're not suggesting that you ask for confidential information only available to potential investors. But there's a lot of public information out there designed to whet the appetite of their potential investors.

In sum, part of what makes franchisees challenging (the fact that they're direct and demanding) is also what makes them able to contribute differently than the typical company-booster on the inside. They can be the perfect balance between Discipline and Innovation, if the company uses them that way.

Section III:
The Next Generation

The Branch of the Future

Washington Mutual recently received a patent from the U.S. Patent & Trademark Office. The thing that makes this patent newsworthy is that it does not protect a product or a specific service. Instead the patent was awarded on the way Washington Mutual structures its branch operations. The patent does not guarantee that Washington Mutual will be profitable – there are financial factors and decisions (for example, hedging strategies) in that sector that can overwhelm local production efforts – but one thing is certain. Obtaining a patent on their branch design generated a buzz within their industry relative to what a branch should look and feel like in the future.

What does the patented branch look like? Go visit one and you'll see. It's friendlier – it encourages people to stop in more regularly. It doesn't feel like a financial institution, it feels more like a Starbucks than a stodgy place where people check their account balances. And it was unique enough in its execution that the company was actually awarded a patent for its concept.

This chapter was written in cooperation with Todd Ordal.

Mr. Ordal served as a Divisional President for Kinko's, where he was responsible for directing the efforts of 6,000 employees in 300 locations. His career there started as a Store Manager.

He has also held executive positions in the sporting goods sector (as CEO of Classic Sport Companies) and in adult learning (as CEO of Dore Achievement Centers).

Mr. Ordal serves as a founding member of the Branch Productivity Institute's BPI Congress.

The commitment to this process says a lot about the vision of Washington Mutual. It also shows where branches are going in the future. There's going to be less of a bright line between retail and B2B. I talked with Todd Ordal about his experience at Kinko's, one of the early pioneers in blending retail and B2B service, and we considered what the branch of the future is going to look like.

FT: Todd, you've held leadership positions in some pretty progressive companies. How has your view of the branch operation changed with your experience?

TO: First of all, I'd like to say that helping to grow a company like Kinko's was very rewarding as well as very humbling. Many things I learned by making mistakes. When I started at Kinko's, we had retail operations whose target customers were business users. But we realized fairly early that even though we operated retail operations, we weren't doing so in a traditional retail way, nor did we look like a standard field sales office. We wanted to create a hybrid Environment that encouraged customer traffic, but remained focused on users whose typical "shopping experience" in their job was more professional than the typical visit to a retail copy shop. We had to do that as we evolved, because you can't place millions of dollars worth of equipment in a location that is going to make five copies at a time.

FT: One of the early challenges I had in writing this book was figuring out what to call our target audience – were they branches, stores, remote sites, field operations? Do you see a great distinction between those groups?

TO: Ten years ago, I would have said, "Yes, they are very different." Today, I think the distinction is blurring as companies consider ways to improve the customer experience. Were we operating stores? Yes. Were they also branches? Yes. Whatever you call your field operations, you can increase their capacity and sales if you address both the retail and the non-retail needs of your target customer. To ignore one or the other leaves money on the table. I was part of the team that spearheaded the tagline, "Your Branch Office" which was kind of a nice way of saying, "This is a branch – but it's your branch".

FT: How will the branch of the future balance the "pull" concept of retailing with the "push" in traditional sales?

TO: Getting started is the hardest part. You often have to dedicate different resources to each channel. The compensation plans, the service standards, the billing expectations can be very different. We started by looking at some other industries that have successfully targeted both the business user and the casual customer, who may become a business user. For the retail operator, they will be forced to consider traditional sales disciplines. For the traditional sales office, it will need to think more about retail concepts like customer traffic and customer experience <u>in their office</u>.

FT: What types of industries did you look to for guidance as you sought to integrate a direct B2B business into your retail stores?

TO: Companies from the largest economic sectors have the most experience with this. Healthcare serves the individual patient <u>as well as</u> the third party payor. Suppliers to the construction industry (for example, lumber yards or mechanical fixture manufacturers) serve both a contractor <u>and</u> a retail component. Transportation segments the 1K flyers and the corporate accounts <u>from</u> the twice-a-year flyer. We wanted to learn from these people – what worked, and as importantly, what didn't. Initially, we were more retail than commercial, but we decided for the good of our customer, it made sense to offer a fuller range of products and services. It took decisive leadership to say, "We're going to be more than just retail."

FT: How did you get started?

TO: Initially we were more opportunistic than strategic. We were committed to retaining the retail customers upon whom we built the business, but this sometimes clashed with large commercial accounts. When a huge commercial job came in, it could overwhelm the entire store if some Discipline wasn't applied to the execution.

FT: How did the employees respond to the migration toward a hybrid operation?

TO: Some people wondered, "What are we?" Are we the place where you get a colored calendar integrating photos of your kids? Are we the "branch office" for a business seeking to expand into a new market? Or are we the extension of the corporate office's document management team? Being a large organization, we wanted to make sure that as we acted in all three of those roles, we presented a consistent face to the market.

FT: How does a company serve different market segments simultaneously without getting lost?

TO: We focused on those elements you talk about as Projective Virtues. We established some consistent parameters around Environment: what should a store look like? We looked at Discipline: what service standards applied across all types of customers. We were committed to balancing Innovation with Discipline; we had to because the company had such a freewheeling spirit in the early days it was a part of our culture. We had to be organized because we were in a process business, but we didn't want the customer's experience to feel like talking to a robot.

FT: How did you promote Innovation?

TO:We used a very flexible rewards system to recognize good ideas. We took the person who had the Idea of the Month and said,"This is heroic – thanks!" We had some general rules about what was out of bounds, but we wanted to encourage free-thinking. In any business, when ideas stop bubbling up, you've got problems. And we started from a good place. In the early days, the managers were highly competitive and highly creative. They didn't worry too much about compliance. As we grew, so did the organizational needs for a bit more system and structure.

FT: Where did most of the good ideas come from?

TO:The field – and I don't think that was unique to Kinko's. I love the story behind the Egg McMuffin. That product came from a suggestion from a McDonald's franchisee in Santa Barbara. Can you imagine McDonald's without the Egg McMuffin today? Or a McDonald's where the Egg McMuffin was only served in Santa Barbara? That's the beauty of a field operation: the best ideas usually come from the field and hopefully there's someone at corporate smart enough to invest in their development.

FT: Let's move from ideas to application. As companies attempt to build branches of the future, what's going to get in their way?

TO: Over-engineering. Here's what I mean by that. Every company goes through a development process. It starts as a creative entity. It has to be creative; to be a challenger or it won't survive in the early days. As it gets larger, it begins to systematize – and in some ways, it has to do that. But some companies go too far: they focus on hiring at a lower and lower level and think they can reach their goals solely though efficiency and compliance.

It takes tremendous leadership to avoid this. You can't have the guy at corporate thinking, "I'm the important one." That attitude leads to entropy (degradation leading to a state of inert uniformity!). Vision gets replaced with financial statements. You'll hear the CFO saying, "if you just cut payroll by 1%, we'll save $7 million." He's right, in the short run. He may be killing your business in the long run. The P&L manager has to be smart enough to address the CFO's valid business concern, without giving up competitive advantage – the manager that can't do that, who caves at every financial question, doesn't deserve to be in a leadership position.

FT: Cost efficiencies do matter. How did you personally achieve them without simply taking a knife to the expense line?

TO: The best way to achieve cost efficiencies is to grow top line revenue. Just hammering on the expense line is very internal-focused. You want to operate efficiently, but according to service measurements, not just expense dollars. Without universal service measurements, the P&L will always win. There are only three things that matter: customer satisfaction, gross margin or bottom line, and top line growth. I'm not saying the P&L doesn't matter – I managed half a billion dollars in annualized revenue at one point. But the service measurements are more important because ultimately they drive the P&L and they answer the question, "What are we trying to do here?"

FT: How will this tie in with the customer message going forward?

TO: It will be at the core. A company that only talks about financial performance internally is hamstrung when discussing service with the customer. The customer today is bombarded with ideas about how to improve their business – and a vendor whose # 1 focus culturally is its own success will not be as creative about providing Innovative customer solutions.

FT: One of the ways we recommend that people look at their branches is to map them on a Branch Productivity Curve, showing which branches are contributors, which are just hanging around and which are losing money. How will the branch of the future be managed?

TO: I love the idea of the visual curve. I think field management will get a lot more visual. Your best field managers understand that running a branch is extremely dynamic: you are never treading water; you're always advancing or retreating. And the only way to build a winning brand is to have highly competitive, dynamic people that are moving their operations in the right direction the vast majority of the time.

I think the branch of the future will be more adept at risk-taking. This is corporate's responsibility: corporate has to put up with some aberrant behavior as the cost of nurturing what you call the Projective Virtue of Innovation.

FT: How will customers' expectations of the branch be changing?

TO: It depends where they are today. If the customer is used to a retail Environment, they may be surprised to be integrated into more traditional sales processes.

FT: Yes, I saw that Honey-Baked Hams is promoting its products directly to businesses as a way for those businesses to reward improving safety in the workplace. So Honey-Baked Hams is now making sales calls in the risk management business!

TO: Exactly, and for those customers used to working with a field sales office – that they never visit, by the way – are going to experience a more retail flavor at a competitor and they'll look at that competitor as an Innovator.

FT: In terms of expanding the B2B customer's perspective to include a retail experience, I know first-hand that it works. I've never had a customer visit one of my traditional offices without eventually giving me an order. And I'm not alone. I spoke with a B2B company that had two customers visit their office over the past six months. When I asked them, "How did it go?" they responded, "Awesome – they had a great time and are using us more often." So if it works twice, why not try it another 200 times?

TO: The branch of the future is not a place to "re-group" after customer meetings. It's the place to have those customer meetings. Talk about a great qualifying step in the sales process: if the customer is willing to make the trip to your office, they are much more likely to buy from you.

FT: Any changes in branch compensation that you would predict?

TO: Each of our branch managers were considered the President of their branch. They didn't get rich off the company stock – they made most of their money off that branch's performance. I think that's the type of incentive that will be required to attract the best people to branch leadership.

And the applicant pool will be improving for a couple reasons: (1) customers are demanding a higher level of business acumen during the sales and service process, which is forcing people to become more knowledgeable, and (2) travel is getting more and more difficult at the same time that technology is making it less necessary: so some highly qualified people that used to be aiming for regional positions are going to step back and say, "How could I make more money as a local field manager - without the headaches of travel?"

FT: As the customer's buying process changes, how will the role of corporate change?

TO: One thing won't change. Corporate's role will continue to be to remove barriers for the field. What will change is the way corporate does that. Technology has put so much more information at the fingertips that corporate can no longer simply be a repository of information – it has to elevate its performance in the areas of analysis and direct action.

Also, with all this information, it is becoming easier to track service levels – and not just within your company. How does a company stack up against its competition? Which regional differences can be explained by economic factors and which cannot?

I also think the role of the Field Manager will become more of a discipline. Sales went through this process, largely through the research and methods introduced by Miller Heiman, over the past several decades. As companies seek growth in same-store sales, improved quality, and enhanced brand, they will come to view site management as a discipline in its own right, just like sales or accounting.

FT: Everybody who enjoys the Dilbert cartoon has a seed planted in their mind that they don't want to work at corporate. What kind of people will be attracted to careers in the branch of the future?

TO:The branch is a great place to start your career – it's where I started mine at Kinko's. But it's not just a start – we had people who made great livings in the field and love the action, the pace, and the responsibility that comes with being on the front line. People who have respect for the customer experience will gravitate to the branch environment – and it won't be by accident.

One byproduct of the changing branch landscape will be that a different type of person will be attracted to corporate as well. Where corporate used to be the place the field went for answers and solutions, making corporate fairly reactive, I believe that field-based decision-making will increase and provide the opportunity for corporate to become much more pro-active in its support of the field.

FT: Corporate will be the place that creates and supports their own Branch University. Corporate will be owned by the branches, rather than vice versa.

TO:That's the kind of corporate I want on my side.

FT: What <u>don't</u> we know about the branch of the future?

TO: We don't know what we don't know.

Everybody thought the ATM was going to put a bunch of tellers on the bread line. But consider how the ATM has really changed branch banking: it's upgraded the level of transaction taking place in those locations. Instead of pulling $50 out of their account, customers are now visiting the bank to discuss cash flow management and investment options. And the bank employee is now handling more sophisticated transactions, on average.

There's a lot we don't know. We don't know exactly how globalization will affect our domestic business practices.

We don't know exactly what impact consumers – and workforces – in emerging markets will have on our systems and processes.

We don't know how security and privacy concerns will affect record-keeping in the branch of the future.

We don't know how well prepared today's branches are for these challenges. And some of them won't make the grade. But those that can communicate across different channels, including B2B and retail, will have the flexibility to adapt to whatever the future brings.

Branching Out: Seven Steps From Idea to Execution

Step One: Understand the Current Risk in your Branch Portfolio

Create a Branch Productivity Curve showing the cumulative performance of your field operations. Note which branches are cumulatively in the Income Production category and which are operating for Speculative purposes. Remember, this is different from simply stating which offices are making money on their own: there are often Speculative Properties that currently make money – they are just not making enough to cover the costs of the remaining organizational infrastructure.

Step Two: Begin to Identify Opportunities for Synchronized Behavior

Identify the common ground in your organization. Is it growing same-store sales? Is it improving quality or reducing waste? Is it enhancing the brand? Something else? This information is used to define those key elements that, when executed synchronously among all locations, will paradoxically create true differentiation in the marketplace. In other words, "Yes your office is different, but here's the part that must be the same."

Step Three: Categorize Obstacles

Using the Periodic Table of Branch Vices as a guide, develop a picture of the problems that currently prevent the organization from reaching its goals. Organize by Root vs. Reflection, Corporate vs. Field.

Step Four: Establish your Model

Using the Branch Productivity Curve, identify the Income-Producing Properties. Working with the people in those operations, specifically define what Virtuosity (the 6 Virtues) looks like for your organization. For example…

- What types of Disciplined behavior do your customers expect or desire from your top field operations? How will you measure compliance with those expectations across all locations?
- What type of Environment would create greater opportunities for your customers and your employees? How will you determine how well that Environment is maintained?
- What commitment will you make to new products and services? How will you develop and test them? What outcome do you desire?
- How important is financial reliability and trust within your business model? How is it recognized and rewarded?
- Beyond financial results, how do you measure the quality of your local teams?
- How do you determine whether you are competitively threatening…or just a doormat for your competitors?

The Model is more than what your best office looks like. It's your definition of success for all markets: "This is what I want us to build here."

Step Five: Define your Campaign

Using your own Periodic Table of Branch Vices, assign deadlines and metrics for reducing or eliminating obstacles to success. Concurrently, assign objectives from Step Four to your Speculative Properties based on their position on the curve. Provide centralized resources and a framework for measurement through Your Branch University.

Step Six: Integrate Recognition & Rewards

Recognize improvements in the Projective Virtues (for example, sales Discipline) and Reward improvements in the Reflective Virtues (for example, meeting sales quota). Link some or all of the payouts to a Company Store, where success generates business resources, not just leisure activities, for the winner.

Step Seven: Understand the Evolution of Risk in your Branch Portfolio

Create a subsequent Branch Productivity Curve showing the cumulative performance of your field operations. Note changes in position on the curve and repeat this cycle, re-allocating resources and responsibilities according to the needs of each field operation or group of operations.

This process will facilitate organizational improvement and reduce misplaced expenditures. More importantly, it will create a class of Professional Field Managers that will better understand – and contribute to – the organization's objectives. This process fundamentally prepares people with local knowledge to see bigger opportunities for the enterprise.

If you think the product is the only thing that matters or that service quality on its own will create sustainable advantage (the "Better Mousetrap" theory), I would ask you to reconsider. The evidence today points toward a clear, sustainable advantage for organizations that consider modeling branch operations a "science" in its own right.

Using this process to develop Branchologists within Your Branch University (where experiments only matter when tied to results – and "tenure" only comes with performance!) will help you find the Discipline, Environment and Innovation that works best for you, your employees – and your customers.

About the Author

The first office Frank Troppe opened as a Branch Manager was recognized by his employer as "Model Office - U.S. Operations." After a 15-year progressive career in field management, Frank founded 3PR Corporation, the first company in the world focusing exclusively on model practices in branch-based businesses.

He is a co-founder of the Branch Productivity Institute and the author of two books. His first book, The Cave Creed, introduces twelve timeless strategies for team-building.

Frank is a graduate of Northwestern University, as well as Loyola University of Chicago Law School. He is a professional speaker and can be reached at info@3prcorp.com.

About the Branch Productivity Institute™

The Branch Productivity Institute is a non-profit organization designed to serve as a community for high-performing branch and store professionals.

Mission: From the branches to the back office, identify and address the organizational issues strategically impacting branch/store-based businesses.

Behind the Mission: There are countless books and strategies on vertical markets (concerns by industry) and functional areas (sales, marketing, management). But "The Branch" is neither fish nor fowl – it's not limited to a particular sector and its needs cross many functional disciplines...branches constitute a diagonal market and it is a significant market - there are over 3,000,000 remote site locations in America alone. These branches and their parent organizations deserve a dedicated focus – and they get one in the Branch Productivity Institute.

Forum & Deliverables: Web-based collaboration that collects and disseminates (1) studies of branch practices, (2) articles by members (co-written by 3PR/BPI where it facilitates faster turnaround), (3) certification opportunities, and (4) independent third-party awards.

Membership: companies join by subscription; individuals join by participation; underwriters join by underwriting studies, conferences, publications, other resources; associations affiliate by cross-membership and joint activities.

Target Participants:

1. **"Top Down"** - Executive leadership in geographically dispersed organizations.
Core benefit: organizational benchmarking through Branch Productivity Index.
2. **"Functional"** - Functional leadership (e.g., VP of sales, marketing, real estate).
Core benefits: opportunity to propose, read, write and/or speak on personally relevant subject matter. Access to Innovation-triggers.
3. **"Trojan Horse"**- Branch Managers, Other Branch Personnel, non-Executive Corporate (Home Office) Personnel.

Core benefit: certification of branch-related skills. Anonymous peer-review and problem-solving, cross-industry perspective.

For more information on how to participate in the establishment and growth of the Branch Productivity Institute, visit www.branchproductivity.com.

Endnotes

1. The words "branch and store" can have very different meanings. Rather than use them interchangeably throughout the work, I will generally refer to all locations operating with remote support as "branches."

2. These vices affect branch performance, but may not necessarily originate in the branch. Some come from corporate!

3. Mark Galloway, CEO of Wire the Market, helped describe this problem in visual form.

4. Coincidentally the three biggest expenses in almost all branch-based models are personnel, real estate and technology.

5. Webster's New Collegiate Dictionary.

6. Selling, General & Administrative expense.

7. One company interviewed required each field vice-president to participate in forecasting conference calls eight (8) times per week, every week. Each call lasted a minimum of 40 minutes. Figure 20 minutes prep time for each call, that's eight hours/week on forecasting. Ouch!

8. See www.cavecreed.com for more information related to Magic Moments.

9. One application of this organization: a company might consider what better serves its needs-Regional Vice-Presidents or Vice Presidents of Income Properties (focusing on defending and increasing those locations Return on Sales) and Vice Presidents of Speculative Properties (focusing on rehabilitation).

10. Recognition comes before Rewards because it is the more important of the two – see the subsequent chapter on R&R for a full discussion.

11. Often, really successful people cannot tell you why they are successful. You hear fairly modest responses like "I work hard. I've got a great team." They've achieved a certain career buoyancy because they are sponges for learning the right things. Breaking down and delivering those right things takes the mystery out of success. These people may not enjoy, or even be effective at, training, but they are a valuable source of what needs to be trained.

12. Just a few years ago, I asked the chairman of a service company, "How do your people feel about the new metrics you've implemented?" Though I doubt he'd say this publicly, he responded, "The people don't matter." His precious metrics showed a 20% revenue hit just one year after that statement.

13. TD Industries, a company in Dallas that is consistently recognized in Fortune Magazine as one of "America's Best Companies to Work For."

14. And fictional!!

15. This is the Projective Virtue of Environment.

16. This is the Projective Virtue of Discipline.

17. This is the Projective Virtue of Innovation.

18. This single question is the basis for an entire business unit within Wire the Market, where our clients pay to receive appointment preparation for their top-performing salespeople. This rewards top-performers by making them look even better on key sales calls and shortens the sales cycle considerably.

19. See The Cave Creed, Frank Troppe, SuccessDNA 2003.

20. People, space and tools are the top three spends in field-based operations! Remember?